# MYTH
# MEMORY
### AND
# MASSACRE

# The Grover E. Murray Studies in the American Southwest

# MYTH
# MEMORY
## AND
# MASSACRE

### THE PEASE RIVER CAPTURE OF CYNTHIA ANN PARKER

**PAUL H. CARLSON AND TOM CRUM**

Texas Tech University Press

This book is typeset in Amasis. The paper used in this book meets the minimum requirements of ANSI/NISO Z39.48-1992 (R1997). ∞

Designed by Kasey McBeath
Maps by Curtis Peoples

Library of Congress Cataloging-in-Publication Data
Carlson, Paul Howard.
Myth, memory, and massacre : the Pease River capture of Cynthia Ann Parker /
Paul H. Carlson and Tom Crum.
p. cm.—(The Grover E. Murray studies in the American Southwest)
Includes bibliographical references and index.
Summary: "Investigates the so-called 'Battle of Pease River' and December 1860 capture of
Cynthia Ann Parker, contending that what became, in Texans' collective memory,
a battle that broke Comanche military power was actually a massacre, mainly
of women. Questions traditional knowledge and historiographic interpretations
of the history of Texas"—Provided by publisher.
ISBN 978-0-89672-707-6 (hardcover : alk. paper) 1. Pease River, Battle of, Tex., 1860.
2. Comanche Indians—Texas—History—19th century. 3. Massacres—Texas—History—
19th century. 4. Parker, Cynthia Ann, 1827?–1864. 5. Texas Rangers—History—
19th century. 6. Indian captivities—Texas. I. Title.
E83.8596.C37 2010
976.4'05--dc22                                    2010020054

Printed in the United States of America
16  17  18  19  20 / 9  8  7  6  5  4

ISBN 978-0-89672-746-5 (paperback)
First paperback printing, 2012

Texas Tech University Press
Box 41037  |  Lubbock, Texas 79409-1037 USA
800.832.4042  |  ttup@ttu.edu  |  www.ttupress.org

With great appreciation, this book is for our wives,
Mary Crum and Ellen Carlson

It has been the misfortune of history,
that a personal knowledge and an
impartial judgment of things rarely
meet in the historian. The best history
of our Country therefore must be the
fruit of contributions bequeathed by
contemporary actors & witnesses,
to successors who will make an
unbiased use of them.

James Madison, 1823

# CONTENTS

**5**

**PETA NOCONA**

# ILLUSTRATIONS

## MAPS

# PREFACE

What most people call the Battle of Pease River occurred along Mule Creek in what is now Foard County, Texas, on December 19, 1860, and resulted in the taking of thirty-four-year-old Naudah—Cynthia Ann Parker—and her very young daughter from their Comanche family and friends. For various reasons the event in the collective memory of Texans became an Indian fight, one that through the years loomed larger and larger. In its retelling it eventually became an engagement in which Comanche military power was broken. In reality, it was little more than a massacre of women and children, most of whom were running away.

The "battle" and the capture of Parker, particularly eyewitness accounts of them, represent the major focus of this study, but the work also deals indirectly with myth, folklore, and memory, both individual and collective. The book is part of a historiographical trend that is changing perceptions of how people view the history of Texas. Through that new historiography a different past is emerging, one usable by a more inclusive society. The new story questions conventional knowledge and historical interpretations that first appeared in the nine-teenth century and played a major role in creating a Texas character and mystique still familiar to most Texans.

As part of the new approach, historians and journalists are chal-lenging traditional interpretations of some of Texas's most cherished events—some of the state's most deeply ingrained historical memories. Among such events, for example, are two from the 1836 defense of the Alamo: William Barrett Travis's alleged line in the dirt, and the death of Davy Crockett. Many such familiar narratives are being reexamined and in the end rewritten in ways that assault a collective memory, folk-lore, and mythology that many Texans hold sacred.

Although the narrative of the Battle of Pease River is not one of the sacred ones, it is similar. In it Texas Rangers and U.S. Cavalry troops attacked a village of Comanches busying themselves with the task of striking camp. As after many such encounters in the nineteenth centu-ry, the victorious participants at Mule Creek embellished the incident, for glory perhaps and maybe to avoid the unpleasant truth that they had killed women and children.

Under normal circumstances the Pease River incident might have been relegated to history's footnotes. Present at Pease River, however, were two notable Texans—Lawrence Sullivan "Sul" Ross and Cynthia Ann Parker—whose prominence inspired an elaborate fabrication of events. Over the next century, resulting stories transformed the indis-criminate slaughter at Mule Creek into a decisive battle, one that not only altered the balance of power in Anglo-Indian warfare across the southern Great Plains but also now resides near the center of Texas mythology. Sul Ross, the twenty-two-year-old Texas Ranger captain who gained additional fame as a Civil War hero and a state senator, became governor of Texas and later president of the Agricultural and Mechanical College of Texas, today's Texas A&M University.

Cynthia Ann Parker, Naudah to her adoptive tribe, was a member of the pioneer clan that erected Parker's Fort in Limestone County, known by Texans for the 1836 Comanche raid in which the then nine-year-old girl was kidnapped and forced for the first time into captivity. At age thirty-four in 1860, she was captured once more, again against her will, which cast a shadow of pathos and tragedy on her repatriation. Filling the space between these violent, bookend encounters is an entire canon of folklore imagining Naudah's life among the Comanches.

While this book treats only the 1860 capture, Parker's episodic biography speaks volumes about the way many Texans have shaped their collective memory. Certain that they had been endowed with a superiority that destined Indians to a secondary fate, Anglos far removed from the action but contemporary to the events remained unconcerned with the methods, such as indiscriminate slaughter, that enforced their superiority. Although Indian atrocities were rarely neglected when accounts of Anglo-Indian warfare were related, the occurrences of Texans' brutality and barbarism were winnowed from most reports and thus eventually forgotten. Such at least is the case in the Battle of Pease River.

All that being so, is there some overarching reason for distinguishing the incident along Mule Creek from other violent encounters, a reason that merits the thorough exegesis that is present here? We think so. Exaggerations are one thing; a complete fabrication of what actually occurred is quite another. Indeed, questionable eyewitness accounts, retold tales, and "histories" associated with the Pease River/Mule Creek incident and the 1860 capture of Cynthia Ann Parker have created a canon of literature heavily based on myth, folklore, and falsehoods. As the conventional history of Texas elsewhere is under siege, now is an appropriate time to reexamine the common but error-filled interpretation of events associated with the Battle of Pease River.

Accordingly, our book has three aims. First, it tries to describe how Sul Ross and his friends shaped descriptions of the battle and the capture of Cynthia Ann Parker for Ross's political ends. Their versions dominated the early telling and retelling of the incidents, and the Ross version, although it changed over the years, by the mid-1880s had become the standard and authorized account. It represented the story Ross wanted disseminated and what many people came to understand as the actual unfolding of the paired events, that is, Texans' collective memory of them.

Second, the book seeks to explain the phenomenon of how a massacre of several women became in our histories a major battle, one that shattered Comanche hegemony. The event, together with the capture of Parker, is celebrated to such an extent that it has become part of Texas myth, folklore, and collective memory. If heritage is defined as what people want to remember, the common story of the Pease River fight and the taking of Cynthia Ann Parker is far more heritage than history.

And, third, as our core message the book attempts to analyze some of the questionable accounts, altered diaries, missing reports, and major questions that have become a part of Parker's life story and histories of the massacre. Both real and alleged participants of events along Mule Creek were familiar with Sul Ross's authorized account, and in later years a few of them questioned the captain's narrative while others used it to embellish their own stories. Historians and journalists have not always studied the pertinent sources carefully or used them wisely, making the source materials a historical problem in need of close examination.

The story of the Battle of Pease River and the 1860 capture of Cynthia Ann Parker is a small one, but it is significant in big ways. It shows how myths loom large in the state's collective memory, it demonstrates the need for a past more usable by a wider range of Texans, and it illustrates how careless errors and simple failure to corroborate evidence play into sustaining mythology, enhancing folklore, and affirming collective memory. As our discussion reveals, not only did inattention and confusion lead to mistakes, but also participants with varying agendas perpetuated errors. In the end, the larger story is a fascinating case study about a confluence of factors and circumstances that have prolonged myth and by extension thwarted a more reliable and accurate Texas past.

We have received much valuable help and assistance in developing the book. Columnist Ken Biffle of the *Dallas Morning News* inspired our initial interest in developing the manuscript. The manner in which he portrayed the Mule Creek incident in one of his popular Texana features raised a number of questions that got us wondering if there was more to the story than the telling revealed. In later stages of working on the manuscript, Judith Keeling of Texas Tech University Press suggested key changes, provided encouragement, and kept us on task.

Many others aided our work. Foremost among them was Ty Cashion of Sam Houston State University. Cashion not only made a number of suggestions that improved the manuscript but also made available resource materials we could not have obtained without his help. To archivists and librarians we also owe a debt of gratitude. Fredonia Paschall, Randy Vance, Monte L. Monroe, Pat Clark, and their assistants at Texas Tech University's superb Southwest Collection provided an enormous amount of support. Curtis Peoples of the Southwest Collection made the maps. John T. "Jack" Becker in Tech's library aided our research, as did people in the interlibrary loan department. Becker also read and critically appraised the manuscript, as did Bryan Edwards and Alwyn Barr, each of whom by discussing and explaining the issues helped us frame and refine our arguments.

Laura K. Saegert and Donaly E. Brice at the Texas State Library in Austin, Casey Edward Greene at the Rosenberg Library in Galveston, Ellen Kuniyuki Brown at the Texas Collection at Baylor University, and Clara Ruddell of the Fort Worth Cultural District Visitors Information

Center each provided information. Warren Striker at the Panhandle-Plains Historical Museum and Jim Bradshaw at the Nita Stewart Haley Memorial Library and J. Evetts Haley History Center also helped. Sarah Ticer and Aryn Glazier at the Dolph Briscoe Center for American History at the University of Texas at Austin were part of a busy group at the research facility who aided our efforts.

Several others provided assistance. They include Cara L. Holtry, librarian at the Cumberland County (Pennsylvania) Historical Society; Amy Castillo on staff in the Mary Couts Burnett Library at Texas Christian University; Margaret Schmidt Hacker, archivist for the National Archives, Fort Worth Branch; Michael T. Meier at the Military History Branch of the National Archives in Washington; Christy Smith, research librarian, Texas Ranger Hall of Fame and Museum in Waco; and Debra Osborne Spindle at the Oklahoma Historical Society.

Jack Selden of Palestine, Steven Butler of Dallas, Gregory R. Campbell of the Department of Anthropology at the University of Montana, and David Sanderford of Granbury provided information. Clark Hitt, Robert Kincaid, and other folks at Crowell, Texas, near the massacre site, also provided suggestions that improved the work.

Don Parker, great-grandson of the former Comanche chief Quanah, camped with one of us on a hill overlooking the massacre site. Don and his father, Baldwin, went with one of us to the site. Both Parkers have noted a spiritual aura of the Mule Creek–Pease River area. Ron Parker, another great-grandson, likewise talked to us about his great-grandfather, about Parker-kin history, about the extensive Parker family who are Comanche, and about the Mule Creek area. Ron Parker also discussed Medicine Mound, a historically strategic hill not far from Mule Creek and a modern-day site of Comanche renewal, and its importance to Comanche identity.

We owe a special thanks to Dr. Joel Lowry of Vernon, Texas, who owns land along Mule Creek where the massacre occurred. Lowry drove from Vernon numerous times to open his ranch and allow us with friends to visit the site and camp there. He was most gracious and helpful.

Two other people deserve special note: our wives, Mary Crum and Ellen Carlson. Mary, especially, has spent more than a few years listening to complaints about wrongheaded sources and differing tales related to the battle and Parker's capture, but both wives have gracefully endured our long hours—even in mountain retreats—of discussing the information, organizing the material, and deciding what to include. We are grateful for their patience and self-sacrifice.

# MYTH
# MEMORY
### AND
# MASSACRE

# 1
## BACKGROUND
## Establishing the Context

H istory and legend often mix. The mixing, writes folklorist B. A. Botkin, "has given rise to a large body of unhistorical 'historical' traditions" and the enactment of "doubtful events [by] historical characters." The popular tale of George Washington cutting down the cherry tree, an event that did not happen, serves as a marvelous illustration of Botkin's reasoning. In Texas, a classic example of Botkin's argument is the apocryphal story of the line drawn in the dirt by William Barrett Travis at the Alamo in 1836. Travis, of course, did not draw any such line, but the dramatic anecdote is so deeply etched in Texans' collective memory that it *must* have happened. In this instance folklore became history.[1]

Indeed, such oft-repeated tales and "bigger-than-life portrayals" helped to create a "mythic nineteenth-century Texas" that was built on a whole series of falsehoods, suggests Sandra L. Myres. It is a mythic Texas, she writes, "perpetuated in art, literature, folklore, and common belief [and] enshrined in many of the history books." Myres concludes,

"If you doubt this check the textbooks used in public schools and colleges." Similarly, Walter L. Buenger and Robert A. Calvert, in the introduction to their book *Texas Through Time: Evolving Interpretations*, write about the myths of various groups of Texans. They note, however, that the dominant culture has created and added to the overarching myths, or traditional knowledge, to the extent that few openly question their premises. The myths have become cherished as sacred. But recently in a whole series of books and articles historians have begun to challenge the myths and conventional beliefs that form the state's collective memory.[2]

One such myth surrounds the 1860 Battle of Pease River. During that brief encounter, Texas Rangers and federal troops forcibly took Naudah (Cynthia Ann Parker) and removed the thirty-four-year-old mother and her young daughter from their Comanche family and friends. Naudah did not see her sons or husband again, and her new life among the extended Parker kin of Texas remained a troubled and unhappy one.

The Pease River story, although muddled, forms a vivid part of the state's collective memory. Its mythic character began soon after the encounter as stories of Parker's "recovery" spread and people exaggerated the battle's magnitude and importance. As early as 1929 Araminta McClellan Taulman, a member of the large Parker family, sent a letter to J. Marvin Hunter, editor of *Frontier Times*. In it she wrote, "I will venture to say that there have been more different erroneous stories written and printed about Cynthia Ann Parker than any person who ever lived in Texas."[3] Taulman may have been right, at least as far as the Battle of Pease River and Parker's 1860 capture are concerned.

The battle—or massacre, really—occurred early on December 19, 1860, a cold, bone-chilling morning. The reports, diary entries, and personal accounts from those involved in the attack vary. Nonetheless, they suggest that fewer than twenty Texas Rangers with twenty federal troops charged into a small Comanche hunting camp along Mule Creek near its junction with the Pease River in modern Foard County. In the village of not more than nine dwellings, approximately fifteen Comanches had been dismantling tepees and packing horses and mules, and when attacked they were moving out of the camp, headed for the Llano Estacado, where they planned to rejoin their families. They were members of a kin-dominated hunting band in the small Noconi (Nokoni) division of the Comanches.

According to at least one participant's account in 1928, the surprise attack was not much of a battle. "I was in the Pease river fight," Texas Ranger Hiram B. Rogers admitted, "but I am not very proud of it. That was not a battle at all, but just a killing of squaws." The early morning strike claimed the lives of "one or two" men, Rogers said, and several women.[4]

The guns-blazing, Hollywood-style attack lasted between twenty and thirty minutes. Most of the Comanche women, because they were running away, in all likelihood were shot in the back. When it was over, the Texas Rangers and federal troops had killed seven Comanches, at least four of them women, and had taken three captives: Cynthia Ann Parker; her daughter, Topsannah (Prairie Flower); and a boy whom Lawrence Sullivan "Sul" Ross, the Ranger captain, took back to Waco and named Pease Ross.[5] Among the Anglo participants there were no casualties, not even minor injuries.

For the Comanches it was a tragic event. In addition to the slaughter and kidnapping, the Anglos also captured about forty horses, destroyed camp equipage, collected many fresh bison hides and robes, and deprived the Indians of tons of meat and lard they needed to survive a winter that had just begun. Although no firsthand Comanche accounts of the battle exist, Comanche oral tradition differs little from the conclusions in this book.[6]

In the Anglo community, at first, except for the capture of Parker, the incident by most measures was a minor clash. As time passed, however, new and sometimes changing accounts and general histories of the episode magnified public perceptions of the fight. In part, they turned a brief, one-sided skirmish into a major battle. Indeed, at least one of the alleged participants, Benjamin F. Gholson, stated that between 150 and 200 warriors were present when the little band of forty white men charged the Indian village, which contained "between 500 and 600" Comanches.[7]

Although not more than forty men were involved in the actual charge through the Comanche village, three separate groups made up the larger expedition. In one, Captain Sul Ross led forty Texas Rangers. In another, First Sergeant John W. Spangler commanded about twenty federal troops from Company H of the Second Cavalry, at the time stationed at Camp Cooper, a military post on the Clear Fork of the Brazos River in Throckmorton County. Captain J. J. "Jack" Cureton led the third group of between seventy and ninety-six militiamen (citizens) from Palo Pinto, Young, and neighboring counties.

Several of the men who were part of the expedition provided reports, wrote diaries, or left reminiscences. Their experiences and perceptions of the fight varied, and understandably in second reports or subsequent descriptions a few of the men left out information that had appeared in earlier statements or added new material. In a more curious instance, someone changed Jonathan H. Baker's diary describing events associated with the expedition. Over a period of nearly thirty years Sul Ross gave at least five separate and sometimes different accounts of the Pease River fight, each of which either Ross or another person recorded. Which accounts should history accept?

Moreover, through an unwitting and, granted, minor error that nonetheless continues to be repeated, the date of the fight, December 19,

1860, got changed to the previous day. The problem with this mistake is that it is now etched in stone: the State of Texas in 1936 engraved the date on a granite historical marker erected near the battle site. It is also the date cited in the articles on Cynthia Ann Parker and Peta Nocona in *The New Handbook of Texas*. The almost universal acceptance of the erroneous date by those who write about the battle is indication of their unquestioned acceptance of a description of events by Sul Ross that became the conventional or authorized account.

The erroneous December 18 date first appeared in 1875. In the early 1870s, Sul Ross wrote a letter to the *Galveston News* in which he used the incorrect date, but for unexplained reasons the letter was not published until June 3, 1875. Two weeks later, on June 19, the same letter appeared in the *Dallas Weekly Herald*. But the date of December 18 is in conflict with an account Ross had given on December 23, 1860, just four days after the massacre, to a correspondent of the *Dallas Herald*. It is also in opposition to Ross's official report of the fight, to a diary entry by militiaman Jonathan Baker, to the eyewitness report of Peter Robertson, to the December 1860 post returns of Camp Cooper, and to the December 24, 1860, and January 16, 1861, military reports of Sergeant Spangler, all of which document the actual date as December 19.[8]

More egregious are the accounts of Benjamin Franklin "Frank" Gholson. Gholson, who most likely was not even a member of the expedition, left at least two sets of reminiscences that refer to the fight. His accounts of the battle along Mule Creek seem incredible, and they vary from those of the other participants to such an extent that their authenticity is suspect. Even if Gholson was present, his faulty description of events renders his testimony nearly inadmissible. Yet many modern histories of the Battle of Pease River and the 1860 capture of Cynthia Ann Parker rely on Gholson's troublesome reminiscences.[9]

Clearly, then, there are varying and strikingly different eyewitness reports of the Pease River fight. As a result of these and other troublesome documents, historians, biographers, journalists, and others working through the various contrasting and sometimes conflicting accounts have produced studies that have created a host of nagging questions. Did Peta Nocona (Puttack), the husband of Cynthia Ann Parker, die in the battle, as some writers maintain? If so, why, in such a society as that of the Comanches, in which gender roles were clear and specific, was Nocona, who was described by Sul Ross, possibly for his own benefit, as "a warrior of great repute," assisting women in butchering game, striking tepees, and packing horses? Or did Puttack live for several more years, as his son Quanah and the respected scout and interpreter Horace P. Jones, who knew Puttack, stated?[10]

As any police investigator will attest, human memory is often unreliable. It shifts and changes, and over time the details of an event become foggy or forgotten. Even the larger picture fades like an old color photo. The mind attaches some hues and tones to its picture in such a way that, as historian David Thelen writes, memory "is constructed not reproduced." Humans, he explains, "reshape their recollections of the past to fit their present needs."[11] Such reshaping muddies much of the story of the Battle of Pease River and the taking of Cynthia Ann Parker.

The story begins in the 1850s on the grassy prairies west of Fort Worth. During that turbulent decade Comanche and Kiowa people on one side and Anglo settlers supported by federal troops, Texas Rangers, and citizen militia groups on the other fought throughout the region, battling over land, livestock, wild game, and rights of occupation. In short, they struggled for control of the large area.

Defined as the region south of the Red River, west of Fort Worth, north of modern Interstate Highway 20, and east of the hundredth meridian, Northwest Texas during the period included what would become approximately twenty counties. Much of the Indian-white antagonism occurred in what are present-day Palo Pinto, Young, Jack, Parker, Stephens, Clay, Archer, and Wichita counties. In the early 1850s the hilly, well-watered, but sometimes drought-stricken prairie country was rich in grass and game, including deer, antelope, and bison. The Red and Brazos rivers, especially the Brazos, and their tributaries drained most of the region. The upper Trinity River, particularly its Clear Fork, drained some eastern parts of the area. Soils in Northwest Texas ranged from sandy loam to gray, black, and red. In 2010 the region remained largely rural, with cattle and horse raising important livelihoods. Crop agriculture included wheat, hay, oats, grain sorghums, and cotton.

Before the 1850s Northwest Texas was a mobile hunting society's paradise. In some ways it was the private hunting preserve of the Comanches and any guests they might indulge. Comanches, Kiowas, and other Indian groups for generations had traveled through, hunted across, lived in, and fought over the region. But now in the 1850s white Texans, farmers mainly, began moving their livestock and farming equipment into the area, threatening the region's hunting potential by disrupting bison herds and tilling up grass. As a result, Indian groups, especially such hunting tribes as the Comanches and Kiowas, found their territory threatened.

The problems were complicated. Through several generations Comanches and others had occupied the area and relied on its rich hunting potential for a livelihood. For reasons both economic and cultural, Comanches could not tolerate the advance of Anglo settlers into their traditional homeland. Conversely, white farmers, ranchers, and townspeople regarded Comanche and Kiowa hunting bands as hostile intruders without legitimate rights to the region.

At the same time, several other issues pressed against the Comanches. A decline in bison numbers, with resulting food shortages;

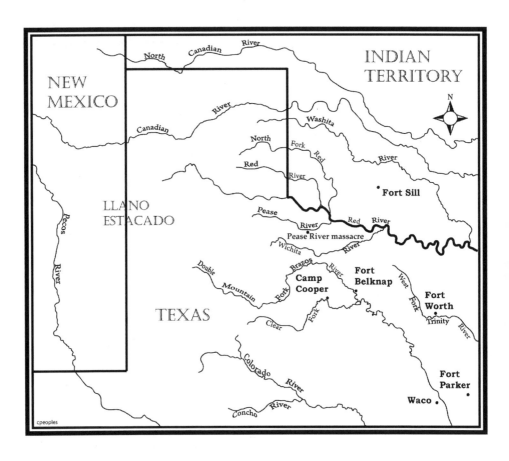

The wide Northwest Texas area, Indian Territory, and the Llano Estacado in 1860.

contraction of their land base; and depopulation from disease and warfare were among them. In fact, after the War with Mexico ended in 1848, all of Comanchería seemed threatened. In Indian Territory (Oklahoma), various well-armed eastern tribes, such as the Osages, pressured the northeastern Comanche divisions. The Fort Smith–Santa Fe Trail cut east and west though the heart of the huge Comanche territory in the Texas Panhandle, and the Cimarron Cutoff of the older Santa Fe Trail further carved up Comanchería. A north-south string of federal forts—Belknap, Phantom Hill, Chadbourne, Concho, McKavett, Terrett, and Clark—built in 1851 and afterward through western Texas from the Red River to the Rio Grande encouraged white settlers to push up against southern Comanchería. In 1853 the federal government negotiated the Fort Atkinson treaties that restricted the reach of the Comanches and other Southern Plains Indians. Beginning in 1858 the Colorado gold rush destroyed once lush hunting grounds in the upper Arkansas River country.[12]

Indeed, the decade of the 1850s represents something of a turning point in Comanche political and economic history. For one thing, the federal government, as in the 1853 Fort Atkinson treaty, was urging Comanches to end their forays into Mexico, thus threatening a source of livelihood and restricting Comanche economic activities. For another thing, the federal military became more aggressive, launching a whole series of offensive operations against Native American homelands. Then, government authorities moved to establish a reservation in Texas, further restricting Comanche hunting, travel, and independence in the state.

Faced with such pressures and confronted by declining bison numbers and concomitant food shortages, Comanches adjusted their raiding practices. Once used to expand territory, to ensure safety through aggression, to gain glory and honor, or to seek revenge, raiding became an economic necessity. Comanches stole horses, cattle, equipment, and other goods, including food, and traded some of it to Comancheros from New Mexico for items tribal members needed. Sometimes Native Americans traded their kidnapped victims. Favorite Comanche-Comanchero trading sites existed in canyons up and down the eastern caprock escarpment of the Llano Estacado.

Comanches were not the only raiders in Northwest Texas. Recent scholarship suggests some, perhaps much, of the supposed Comanche raiding activity was actually the dirty work of white thugs, desperados, and thieves falsely identified as Native Americans.[13] Regardless, whites struck back against Indians, attacking Comanche, Kiowa, and Wichita camps in Texas. They even raided Indian villages located north of the Red River in Indian Territory, a region outside the jurisdiction of Texas state troops.

With a view to ending the conflicts and perhaps treating Native Americans fairly, the federal government stepped in. The Fort Atkinson Treaty, among other things, provided food and clothing to Comanches. In Northwest Texas the federal government established two reservations. One housed Wichitas, Tonkawas, Caddoes, and others deemed "friendly." Their reserve, the Lower or Brazos Indian Reservation, of about 37,000 acres, opened in 1855 just below the junction of the Clear and Salt forks of the Brazos River in Young County. The second reservation housed at first about 277 Texas Comanches (Penatekas), but its population soon increased to over 500. Their reserve of 22,000 acres, the Upper or Comanche Reservation, stood some forty-five miles farther west along the Clear Fork of the Brazos near the boundary of modern Shackelford and Throckmorton counties. It also opened in 1855, and the federal government located Camp Cooper there.[14] Major Robert S. Neighbors, who had helped survey sites for the reserves, became the government's supervisor for the twin projects. Shapley P. Ross, the father of Sul Ross and a former Texas Ranger, became agent at the Lower Reservation, and John R. Baylor, a former state legislator and lawyer, was agent for the Upper Reservation before authorities in 1857 replaced him with Matthew Leeper.

The reservations did little to stop Indian and Anglo difficulties in Northwest Texas. Raids and counterattacks continued. Murder, kidnapping, and theft often occurred when Indians or white thugs raided ranches, farms, and outlying settlements. White counterstrikes sometimes led to attacks against innocent villagers, with all Indian men, women, and children becoming targets. In addition, Anglo desperados and horse thieves, some of them from Central Texas, raided ranches and reservations indiscriminately. Some of the horse thieves rode across the Red River into Indian Territory, stole Indian horses, and drove them into Texas to sell. Sometimes they stole from Anglo farmers and ranchers and then sold the animals back to the very people whose horses they had taken earlier. Such horse thieves, if caught with Indian horses, were rarely punished in Texas.

Moreover, John Baylor, bitter over his dismissal as Indian agent, became an enemy to Robert Neighbors and the Comanches who had asked for his removal. In his newspaper, *The White Man*, published first in Jacksboro and later in Weatherford, he condemned Comanche attacks and exaggerated Indian atrocities. He pursued the resignation of Neighbors, demanded the reservations be closed, and sought leadership of a Texas Ranger regiment. He stirred up plenty of anti-Indian sentiment, which, because of increased raiding after 1855, proved an easy task.

In April 1858, Native Americans, thought to be Comanches, with at least four white men raided farms and ranches in Jack County. They stole horses, killed several members of the James B. Cambren and Tom Mason families, robbed several houses, and kidnapped and later killed other settlers before fleeing. The white desperadoes, who had taken a thousand dollars from a trunk in the Cambren home, headed south. The Indians rode north across the Red River. Authorities later caught four of the white thieves.[15]

About the same time, April 1858, Captain John S. "Rip" Ford raised a Texas Ranger company to move against Comanches. Under orders from Governor Hardin R. Runnels, Ford signed up 102 men, and with 113 Indian auxiliaries under Shapley Ross he moved north from a camp near the junction of Hubbard's Creek and the Clear Fork of the Brazos in Stephens County. The combined force crossed the Red River into Indian Territory near modern Davidson, Oklahoma, turned northwest, and rode through modern Greer and Roger Mills counties. They were far outside Ranger jurisdiction, looking for a large Noconi Comanche village believed to be near the picturesque Antelope Hills.

About mid-May, scouts discovered a Tenawa Comanche village of seventy lodges along Little Robe Creek just north of the Canadian River. The Noconi camp, their intended goal, was several miles up the Canadian. Nonetheless, early the next day, May 12, Ford's Texas Rangers and their Indian allies attacked. Catching the Tenawas off guard, the Rangers succeeded in killing many warriors and taking women and children prisoners. Unfortunately for Ford, the battle dragged on past noon, which gave warriors from the Noconi camp time to come to the aid of the Tenawas.

Although Ford's men were now heavily outnumbered and their horses jaded, Ford regrouped them and ordered a charge on the new arrivals. A running fight followed, but with tired mounts Ford's Rangers could not fully engage the enemy, and about two o'clock in the afternoon Ford called a halt. His men and horses were exhausted, at least two of his men were dead, three of them were wounded, and he had received reports of a third, and larger, Penateka Comanche hunting camp under Potsanaquahip (Buffalo Hump) twelve miles down the Canadian River.

It was time to leave. Ford ordered his company back across the Canadian, and after crossing, the men rode about a dozen miles before going into camp. The next morning, May 13, Ford with his Texas Rangers and Shapley Ross with his reservation Indians started home. Ten days later, having abandoned their wagons and some of their equipment and facing food shortages, they were back at their camp along the Clear Fork.[16]

The Battle of Little Robe Creek had been a rout. Ford's mixed group of fighters had ridden over three hundred miles, fought for almost seven continuous hours, and suffered only a few casualties while inflicting heavy damage on the Comanches. They captured nearly three hundred horses and took several prisoners, mainly women and children. The battle also showed how whites might carry the fight into the heart of Indian country.

Unfortunately, the Ford-Ross Canadian River expedition had struck innocent people, not the warriors operating in small marauding bands whom they had hoped to subdue. The small raiding bands could not be punished by dramatic, long-distance forays, which resulted only in attacks on innocent women and children in their homes. From the point of view of Texans living in the vicinity of the Brazos River reservations, however, the Little Robe Creek battle was a great victory and demonstrated the advantages of an aggressive offensive campaign against Comanches.

General David E. Twiggs, commanding the Department of Texas, liked the idea of an offensive campaign deep into Comanche territory. He thought such an operation would cut Indian raiding in Texas. Accordingly, upon receiving War Department approval for such an operation, Twiggs selected Earl Van Dorn, a West Point graduate from Mississippi, to lead an expedition. Van Dorn, captain of Company A, Second U.S. Cavalry, was stationed with his company at Fort Belknap in Young County.

Captain Van Dorn's force included Companies A, F, H, and K of the Second Cavalry, a detachment from the First U.S. Infantry, and some Caddoes, Tonkawas, and Delawares from the Lower Brazos Reservation. Important for the story presented here, Sul Ross, the nineteen-year-old son of Indian agent Shapley P. Ross, led the 135 Indian auxiliaries. Van Dorn counted 300 men in his command.

The expedition left Fort Belknap on September 15, 1858, and headed north across the Red River to establish a supply base on Otter Creek just west of the Wichita Mountains. Named Camp Radziminski, the post served as a base of operations, with infantry soldiers manning it. Not long after his men had established the camp, Tonkawa and Caddo scouts found a contingent of hungry Comanches camped next to a Wichita village at Rush Creek on the Washita River, some seventy-five or more miles to the east. The Comanches were there at the invitation of the Wichitas and on their way to or—depending upon whom you read—from a peace conference with federal authorities at Fort Arbuckle, just north of the Arbuckle Mountains.[17]

The Comanche camp numbered 120 lodges. Among the experienced warriors present were Buffalo Hump, the Penateka headman, and Yamparika leaders Quahateme (Hair Bobbed on One Side) and Hotoyokowat (Over the Buttes). Members of other Comanche divisions gathered close by, as they did nearly every autumn, to engage in trade and general exchange. Because of the peace talks, no one expected trouble; consequently, they did not post guards for either their camp or their large horse herds.

Captain Van Dorn, in the meantime, advanced his men hard toward the camp, and early on October 1, 1858, they struck. Sul Ross and his reservation Indians drove off the Comanches' horses, forcing the warriors to fight on foot. Second Cavalry troopers rode with guns blazing into the village. They killed many Indians, burned lodges and camp equipage, and drove the Comanches into the ravines and draws of the area. The Comanches on foot fought back as best they could, killing five soldiers and wounding others.

Sul Ross was among the wounded. He had taken an arrow in his arm, and a Comanche identified as Mohee (possibly Muhy, who signed an 1838 Texas treaty) shot him "point blank" in the side but did not kill him. According to Ross's biographer, Judith Ann Benner, Mohee was a person Ross "had known since childhood." Mohee was about to scalp Ross, but he turned away, distracted by his chief. Before he could continue, Lieutenant James P. Major killed him.[18] If Mohee died, one must wonder, writes Thomas Kavanagh, about the "Comanche named Mohee" reported two months later "to be near the Texas Reservation."[19]

The Wichita village fight was significant on several levels. For the diminishing Comanche empire in the 1850s it represented another decisive defeat that appeared to augur the tribe's complete unraveling: some fifty-eight people dead, 120 lodges burned, supplies destroyed, and their horse herd gone. As Stan Hoig writes, "The Comanches had seen the safety of their homes and camps in Indian Territory violated by a surprise and, to their mind, unwarranted attack." Demoralized, Comanches retreated to the north and west and into the plains and canyonlands of the Texas Panhandle and the Llano Estacado.[20]

For the Wichitas it was also costly. Van Dorn's command stole their vital corn supplies. As a result, the Wichitas left their valley homes and sought help at Fort Arbuckle. Moreover, believing the attack came as a result of the Comanche presence, the Wichitas became embittered, and the tribes renewed their old feuds, at least for a time.

For federal troops, especially the Second Cavalry, the battle marked the first of several subsequent forays against Southern Plains Indians. Operations and attacks similar to the Wichita village strike continued for two more years before the Civil War drew troops away. In 1859, for example, Captain Van Dorn led several expeditions through Indian Territory. On at least one occasion he and his troops moved north into Kansas to carry the fight to northern Comanches.

For Sul Ross the Wichita village fight provided some military experience and a bit of acclaim, at least in Texas. Earl Van Dorn's report appeared in local newspapers, and other participants mentioned Ross's role in the fight. The accolades got him an offer, which he declined, of a military career as an officer. John H. Reagan spoke about Ross in a speech in the House of Representatives. Ross also gained the attention of people in Northwest Texas, where, despite the success of Ford's Canadian River campaign and Van Dorn's Wichita village fight, raiding continued.[21]

Through 1859 and 1860 the Northwest Texas region swirled into chaos, or so it seemed. Conditions worsened, lawlessness increased, vigilante groups formed, and Native Americans and Anglo desperadoes raided ranches, farms, and exposed homesteads. They made life difficult for the new Anglo arrivals. In fact, many farming people retreated from the semiarid land, where few nineteenth-century farmers should have been.

John Baylor, still embittered about his dismissal from the reservation, became more aggressive. He continued to blame Anglo-Indian troubles on Comanches and other Indians of the two Brazos River reserves, to exaggerate the hostilities, and to call for closing the reservations. He organized militia units to waylay Indians who might enter or leave the reservations, sent marauding gangs onto the reserves, and pressured authorities for protection against Indian raiding.[22] Finally, to protect the reservation Indians, Robert Neighbors recommended closing the Brazos reserves and removing Native Americans from Texas. Federal authorities agreed, and sometime before August 1, 1859, the Comanches of the Texas reservation departed for Indian Territory.

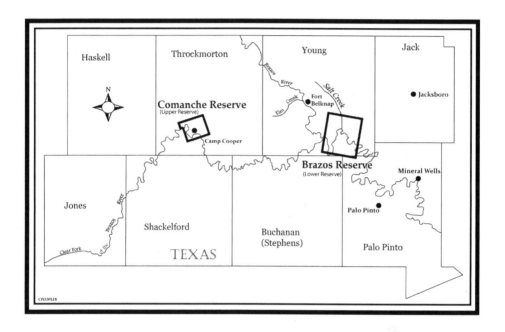

Texas Indian reservations at closing in 1859.

General John R. Baylor in his Confederate uniform, ca. 1863. Courtesy of
William A. Keleher Pictorial Collection No. 000-742, Center of
Southwest Research, University Libraries, University of
New Mexico, Photo 000-742-0014.

But raiding continued. In response, Captain Van Dorn's Second Cavalry pounded Comanche villages where it could find them, and various citizen groups struck Indian camps. Then, in March 1860, Governor Sam Houston authorized Colonel Middleton T. Johnson, a former Texas Ranger from Tarrant County, to raise a state Ranger force. He was, writes Judith Benner, "to 'pursue and punish' . . . Indians then ravaging the . . . northwestern settlements of the state."[23]

Five companies answered Johnson's call. The companies, one of which Captain J. M. Smith raised in Waco, made their way to Fort Belknap and, joined by two additional companies, on May 18 mustered on the parade ground. During the muster Captain Smith became lieutenant colonel under Johnson. Thereupon, the Waco company elected the much acclaimed Sul Ross, only twenty-one years old, their captain.

Not all was well. Ross, not fully recovered from his injury at the Wichita village, was ill and spent several days in bed absent from Fort Belknap. Colonel Johnson left the post for Galveston temporarily. Days passed without movement against the Comanches. The Texas Rangers, idle and bored, complained about water, rations, Ranger policies, and sorry leadership. When the men found a stash of whiskey, military discipline disappeared amid quarrels, fights, and mounting criticism, some of it aimed at Ross.

Once in the field, a different problem ensued. Getting word that a Texas Ranger force of three hundred men was moving north across the Red River to strike their villages, Comanches and Kiowas ignited the prairies. Fires raged out of control, and much of western Indian Territory between the Red and Arkansas rivers burned, leaving Johnson's Texas Rangers, including Ross's Waco company, unable to operate effectively. On August 26, 1860, Johnson's Texas Ranger regiment disbanded.[24]

In the meantime, in Parker, Palo Pinto, Young, and other counties of Northwest Texas raiding continued. Citizens complained to Governor Houston. Led by John Baylor, many people in Parker County blamed the raids on Comanche or Kiowa transgressors and on the failure of Johnson's Ranger force, including Sul Ross's first Texas Ranger command. To stop the marauding and appease area citizens, Houston asked Sul Ross to organize another Texas Ranger company. He wanted sixty volunteers. Ross agreed in mid-September and quickly filled his command in Waco. He headed for Fort Belknap, where he arrived on October 17, 1860.[25]

John Baylor and his followers were not happy, for Baylor wanted to lead such a force. To protest the Ross appointment, citizens of Palo Pinto County held a barbecue for Baylor, and some people in attendance passed a petition asking for Sul Ross to resign his captaincy so that Baylor might replace him. Eighty people signed the document. Sul Ross, young but seasoned and experienced, ignored the petition and went about his duties. He organized his command, kept scouting patrols constantly in the field, and moved his Rangers to intercept marauders.

The Rangers missed some Indians. Late in the fall, during a cold, wet, rainy spell, Comanches apparently of the small Noconi division moved past the thin line of Ross's defense and struck. About fifty-five warriors rode through the Northwest Texas settlements looking for horses and raising havoc. For three days, November 26 through November 28, they passed through Jack, Parker, and Palo Pinto counties, stealing horses, killing settlers, confiscating or destroying household equipment, and taking scalps and captives. Among their victims were members of five families who lived in the Jacksboro, Weatherford, and modern Mineral Wells vicinities, including the James Landman, Calvin Gage, John Brown, William Eubanks, and Ezra Sherman families.

Sherman owned a small cabin on Staggs Prairie near the outskirts of modern Mineral Wells.

The Comanches left with an estimated three hundred horses and three prisoners. Shortly afterward they released two of the captives, who were teenage girls, and later they killed the third prisoner, a boy. While in the settlements they had killed at least six people, wounded several others, and scalped two women. They had removed ticking from several beds, collected other material they could carry on their horses, and took Martha Sherman's Bible, which one of the warriors planned to use for backing on his shield.[26]

Settlers were scared. As Rupert Richardson wrote, "Terror seized the land; farm and ranch operations were discontinued; and in villages no business was transacted. Not a few people fled the country." They were also angry, and this time they would not let the raiders go unpunished. Men from Palo Pinto, Parker, and adjoining counties created a militia force; elected J. J. "Jack" Cureton, a seasoned frontiersman, as captain; and assembled in Loving's Valley along the Palo Pinto–Jack County line.[27]

Sul Ross and his Texas Rangers also responded. Ross had established a permanent camp in October several miles west of Fort Belknap at a site along Elm Creek. There about December 11 twenty federal troopers of Company H, Second Cavalry, from Camp Cooper, under Sergeant John W. Spangler, joined him. Two days later the Ross and Spangler companies met Cureton and his militiamen along Salt Creek in Young County north of Fort Belknap.

On December 14 the combined command moved out. Captain Ross, having been forced to leave some men behind on account of the poor condition of their mounts, led forty Texas Rangers. Among them were First Lieutenant Thomas H. Kelliher; Second Lieutenants M. W. Somerville and David L. Sublett; Private James Ireland; Surgeon S. L. Nidelett;

and Antonio "Anton" Martinez, Ross's Mexican cook who once had been a captive of the Comanches.

Captain Cureton's militia unit counted about ninety men, nearly all of them on tired and worn horses. Among the men was First Sergeant Jonathan H. Baker, a schoolteacher from Palo Pinto who kept a diary of the company's actions. Charles Goodnight, who became a major Texas Panhandle cattleman and later reported his recollections of the campaign, scouted for the militiamen. Like Goodnight, Peter Robertson, who also served as scout, left reminiscences about his role in the expedition, as did Francis M. Peveler. C. C. Slaughter, who later became one of the state's most successful ranchers and bankers, joined the Cureton militia.[28]

Sergeant Spangler had twenty federal cavalrymen with him, and the principal scout for the expedition was a man named Stewart. Sul Ross and Peter Robertson refer to him as Mr. Stewart, and some other members of the expedition who left accounts of the fight write his name as Tom Stewart, Tom Stuart, or Jim Stuart. Still others called him John Socie, a mixed-blood bison hunter.

The combined command followed Salt Creek, its destination a Noconi Comanche village somewhere up the Pease River. A few days earlier, Ross had heard that Indians were in the vicinity of the upper Pease. The information had come from Goodnight and "a rancher and lawyer of the frontier" named W. J. Mosely, who in early December had led a small party of citizens up the Pease. They turned back before any engagement had occurred.[29]

As the Ross command moved forward, problems developed. The poor condition of the citizens' mounts slowed their progress, and they lagged behind the Texas Rangers and the federal soldiers. More serious was forage for the animals. Grass along the line of travel was thin at best, forcing the horses, already in poor condition, to subsist on cottonwood bark and "dry sedge." By December 16 several miles separated

Cureton's men from the Rangers and federal troopers, and Ross had been forced to send back some of his men with horses that were giving out.[30]

When it reached the Pease River on December 17, the command turned west and traveled up the wide, shallow stream about four or five miles before stopping. That night Cureton's men camped several miles below the others, for their horses, and perhaps their own inexperience, had slowed their progress.

Two days later, on the morning of December 19, 1860, Sul Ross and John Spangler spied the Noconi village they had been seeking from a prominence about two hundred yards away. The village, located along Mule Creek just up from its confluence with the Pease River, was a tiny hunting camp composed of nine dwellings. On this cold morning about fifteen Comanches, mostly women and children, were packing horses and preparing to depart. Some of them, in fact, were already mounted.

Fearful they might be seen and worried the Comanches might flee, Ross ordered an attack. Spangler and his twenty troopers swept to the right to cut off a retreat, and Ross with not more than twenty Texas Rangers charged on the left and into the camp. The Comanches had no chance. The attack and subsequent massacre were over in less than thirty minutes. There are conflicting reports about the number of Indian casualties, but Ross reported twelve dead and three captured. Spangler reported fourteen Indians killed. Jonathan Baker, the diarist, after two days of searching for Comanche bodies, reported the Rangers and troopers had killed seven people, four women and three men. A few Comanches on good horses made their escape, or perhaps as Jonathan Baker claims, Sergeant Spangler let some Indians get away. The command captured about forty Indian ponies and suffered no casualties, although two horses suffered wounds.[31]

The three Comanche captives included a boy and a woman with her baby daughter. Ross took the boy back to Waco and named him Pease Ross. He lived for a time with the Ross family slaves and married a slave owned by Neil McLennan. Sul Ross gave him an opportunity to return to the Comanches but he chose to remain in McLennan County. The woman, of course, was Cynthia Ann Parker. Although the soldiers saw that she was a white woman, her identity remained a mystery until after she and the federal troops reached Camp Cooper several days later and many miles from the scene of the battle. Parker's daughter, Topsannah (meaning Prairie Flower) died a few years later, but Parker lived at least until 1870, when the federal census for Anderson County listed her as forty-five years old and living in the household of her sister, Orlena Parker O'Quinn.[32]

In his diary Baker indicates that after the attack Ross and his men returned down the Pease River and met Cureton's civilian command moving upstream on the opposite side. The militiamen, disappointed in not participating in the fight, continued to the village, or what was left of it. They decided to remain in the area a few more days to search for additional Indian camps. Ross with his Texas Rangers and Spangler with his federal troops also camped near the battle site that night. The next morning, December 20, Ross and Spangler started back toward Fort Belknap, where on December 23 Ross gave an account of the engagement to a correspondent of the *Dallas Herald* before continuing to his permanent camp on Elm Creek. Spangler rode on to Camp Cooper, taking Parker and her eighteen-month-old baby with him.[33]

The incident along Mule Creek was hardly a battle. It was not fought against a much larger force, and it came at a time when Comanche political society and military strength were in retreat. In 1860 Comanche power was only a shadow of its former status. The American Civil War, which turned Anglo attention in a different direction, would give the Comanches a reprieve, of sorts, just as improving rainfall would replenished sparse grassland and allow bison numbers to stabilize or even increase and thus ease Comanche food shortages temporarily. Their political and economic vitality, however, did not enjoy a concomitant resurgence.

During the 1860s reports of the Mule Creek incident began to circulate across the state. Many of the participants, however, did not record their accounts until after the turn of the twentieth century. Nonetheless, partly because of the capture of Parker, a member of a large and prominent Texas family, and partly as a result of the growing political ambitions of Sul Ross, the massacre grew in importance in the state's collective memory. Indeed, it grew until it became a fight and then a major battle, one that allegedly destroyed Comanche power in Texas.

In this case, however, there is more to mythmaking than Ross's political dreams or Parker's return to Anglo civilization. In the Battle of Pease River, as in other such Indian-Anglo encounters in Texas and the larger American West, the victorious participants embellished the incident and their role in it. They discounted their own atrocities and reported the fight in ways that demonstrated their superiority over a vanquished enemy. Anglo Texans far removed from but contemporary with the incident gloried in news of a battle that affirmed their own preeminence and from their viewpoint assisted in securing a violent land from a savage foe. Thus, the Pease River massacre helped shape the collective memory of Texas and its mythic nineteenth-century past.

# 2
## THE SOURCES
## Participant Accounts

A people's perception of their history is often formed not so much from an understanding of the facts as from conventional knowledge passed on to them through myth and folklore. Indeed, Francis Abernethy, former executive secretary-editor of the Texas Folklore Society, has defined folklore as the traditional knowledge of a culture. The Alamo's line-in-the-dirt myth represents an example of that definition. In other words, many people are more familiar with folklore's rendition of a historical event than they are with the actual event.[1]

Such misunderstanding informs the standard of "truth" in the Battle of Pease River. In this case, the indiscriminate killing of mainly women along Mule Creek became a valiant affair, a heroic and famous Texas Ranger victory over a superior Comanche force. The capture of Cynthia Ann Parker, the subsequent rise to prominence of her son Quanah, and the growing political ambitions of Lawrence Sullivan "Sul" Ross each merged in the late nineteenth century to transform the incident in the state's collective consciousness from a massacre to a major engagement. Moreover, as time passed, the collective memory of Texans demanded that the 1860 event, one seemingly fraught with significance, be worthy of becoming part of the Texas mystique.

Some reports from the participants were keys to perpetuating the myth. Some of them represent reliable sources. Some were embellished, some altered, and some just fictitious. Nonetheless, the Pease River narratives and the secondary literature based on them are responsible for turning the massacre into a great battle. They need to be examined.

For clarity, the eyewitness narratives can be divided into three categories. One comprises the reports of Texas Rangers Sul Ross, Hiram B. Rogers, and Benjamin C. Dragoo. The two reports of Benjamin Franklin "Frank" Gholson, who claims he was a Ranger at the Pease River battle, deserve and receive more detailed attention in a subsequent chapter. A second category includes the accounts from men in Captain J. J. "Jack" Cureton's militia command, particularly those of Peter Robertson, Jonathan Hamilton Baker, Francis Peveler, and Charles Goodnight. In the third category are the two military reports of First Sergeant John W. Spangler of the U.S. Cavalry.

## The Texas Ranger Reports

While we review Sul Ross's several versions of the Pease River battle later in greater detail, in this chapter we quote his most common report in full. Even though it was his fifth account and published twenty-six years after the attack, its lengthy narrative is highly significant in how it informs the widely accepted interpretation of events at Mule Creek. It is the foundation on which Texans' collective memory of the battle and the capture of Cynthia Ann Parker is constructed.

First appearing in print in James T. DeShields's 1886 book *Cynthia Ann Parker*, this common Ross story, although drawn at best from faulty

James T. DeShields, ca. 1890. Courtesy of DeGolyer Library,
Southern Methodist University, Dallas, Texas, A1991.1750

memory and often embellished, became the authorized account, the version he and his political friends wanted disseminated as broadly as possible. They were successful. It is now cited and used in many articles and books and here serves as a measuring rod against which other reports of the Pease River events are examined.

On the 18th of December, 1860, while marching up Pease river, I had some suspicions that Indians were in the vicinity, by reason of the buffalo that came running in great numbers from the north towards us, and while my command moved in the low ground, I visited all neighboring high points to make discoveries. On one of these sand hills I found four fresh pony tracks, and being satisfied that Indian videtts [sic] had just gone, I galloped forward about a mile to a higher point, and riding to the top, to my inexpressible surprise, found myself within 200 yards of a Comanche village, located on a small stream winding around the base of the hill. It was a most happy circumstance that a piercing north wind was blowing, bearing with it clouds of sand, and my presence was unobserved and the surprise complete. By signaling my men as I stood concealed, they reached me without being discovered by the Indians, who were busy packing up preparatory to a move. By this time the Indians mounted and moved off north across the level plain. My command, with the detachment of the Second Cavalry, had out-marched and become separated from the citizen command, which left me about sixty men. In making disposition for attack, the sergeant and his twenty men were sent at a gallop, behind a chain of sand hills, to encompass them in and cut off their retreat, while with forty men I charged. The attack was so sudden that a considerable number were killed before they could prepare for defense. They fled precipitately right into the presence of the sergeant and his men. Here they met with a warm reception, and finding themselves completely encompassed, every one fled his own way, and was hotly pursued and hard pressed.

The chief of the party, Peta Nocona, a noted warrior of great repute, with a young girl about fifteen years of age mounted on his horse behind him, and Cynthia Ann Parker, with a girl child about two years of age in her arms and mounted on a fleet pony, fled together, while Lieut. Tom. Killiheir and I pursued them. After running about a mile Killiheir ran up by the side of Cynthia's horse, and I was in the act of shooting when she held up her child and stopped. I kept on after the chief and about a half a mile further, when in about twenty yards of him I fired my pistol, striking the girl (whom I supposed to be a man, as she rode like one, and only her head was visible above the buffalo robe with which she was wrapped) near the heart, killing her instantly, and the same ball would have killed both but for the shield of the chief, which hung down, covering his back. When the girl fell from the horse she pulled him off also, but he caught on his feet, and before steadying himself, my horse, running at full speed, was very nearly on top of him, when he was struck with an arrow, which caused him to fall to pitching or "bucking," and it was with great difficulty that I kept my saddle, and in the meantime, narrowly escaped several arrows coming in quick succession from the chief's bow. Being at such disadvantage he would have killed me in a few minutes but for a random shot from my pistol (while I was clinging with my left hand to the pommel of my saddle) which broke his right arm at the elbow, completely disabling him. My horse then became quiet, and I shot the chief twice through the body, whereupon he deliberately walked to a small tree, the only one in sight, and leaning against it, began to sing a wild, weird song. At this time my Mexican servant, who had once been a captive with the Comanches and spoke their language as fluently as his mother tongue, came up, in company with two of the men. I then summoned the chief to surrender, but he promptly treated every overture with contempt, and signalized this declaration with a savage attempt to thrust me with the lance, which he held in his left hand. I could only look upon him with pity and admiration. For, deplorable as was his situation, with no chance of escape, his party utterly destroyed, his wife and child captured in his sight, he was undaunted by the fate that awaited him, and as he seemed to prefer death to life, I directed the Mexican to end his misery by a charge of buckshot from the gun which he carried. Taking up his accoutrements, which I subsequently sent Gov. Houston to be deposited in the archives at Austin, we rode back to Cynthia Ann and Killiheir, and found him bitterly cursing himself for having run his pet horse so hard after an "old Squaw." She was very dirty, both in her scanty garments and her person. But as soon as I looked on her face, I said, "Why, Tom, this is a white woman, Indians do not have blue eyes." On the way to the village, where my men were assembling with the spoils, and a large *caballada* of "Indian ponies," I discovered an Indian boy about nine years of age, secreted in the grass. Expecting to be killed, he began crying, but I made him mount behind me, and carried him along. And when in after years I frequently proposed to send him to his people, he steadfastly refused to go, and died in McLennan county last year.

After camping for the night Cynthia Ann kept crying, and thinking it was caused from fear of death at our hands, I had the Mexican tell her that we recognized her as one of our own people, and would not harm her. She said two of her boys were with her when the fight began, and she was distressed by the fear that they had been killed. It so happened, however, both escaped, and one of them, "Quanah" is now a chief. The other died some years ago on the plains. I then asked her to give me the history of her life with the Indians, and the circumstances attending her capture by them, which she promptly did in a very sensible manner. And as the facts detailed corresponded with the massacre at Parker's Fort, I was impressed with the belief that she was Cynthia Ann Parker. Returning to my post, I sent her and child to the ladies at Cooper, where she could receive the attention her situation demanded, and at the same time dispatched a messenger to Col. Parker, her uncle, near Weatherford, and as I was called to Waco to meet Gov. Houston, I left directions for the Mexican to accompany Col. Parker to Cooper in the capacity of interpreter. When he reached there, her identity was soon discovered to Col. Parker's entire satisfaction and great happiness.[2]

Thus reads the oft-cited Ross account. For important political reasons that will become clear, it mentions neither the number of Native Americans present at Mule Creek nor the sex of the Indians killed there.

Hiram B. Rogers was a member of the company of Texas Rangers involved in the Pease River incident. He had joined the Ross command October 3, 1860, and accepted his discharge on February 5, 1861. Rogers received $102.50 for his service. In 1928, J. A. Rickard interviewed

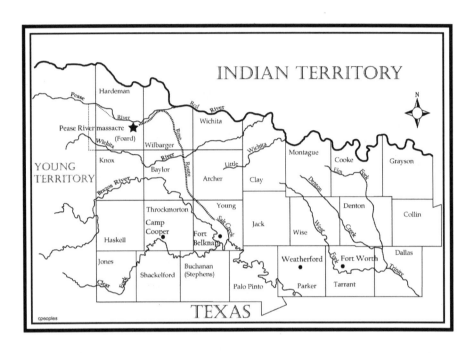

Northwest Texas in 1860, showing route to Comanche hunting camp along Mule Creek.

Rogers at the former Ranger's home near Chalk Mountain, Texas. Eighty-nine years old at the time of the interview, he wandered through topics during his conversation, and Rickard struggled to keep an accurate record of the exchange. To his credit, Rogers was one of only two persons, Ben Dragoo the other, who admitted he might be wrong about some details of the long-past Pease River events.[3]

During the interview Rogers made a number of pertinent statements. He said John Socie, a Choctaw Indian, was the guide. The Texas Rangers' horses were very poor. They had to cut cottonwood bark to feed them. Captain Cureton's militia company was not in the fight because of the condition of their horses, and it took them four hours to get to the scene of the fight. The fight was on Mule Creek. One or two men and sixteen women were killed, he said. Quanah, Cynthia Ann Parker's son, was there, but escaped on one of the prettiest horses Rogers ever saw. "Mexican Louie," he said, killed Nocona, Parker's Comanche husband, in a little grove of trees. As far as Rogers knew, Parker did not see Nocona's body. The captured Indian boy, he noted, said there were only seventeen men among the Comanches. The Ross party captured fifty-nine horses and one gray mule. The most memorable sentence in the interview has Rogers saying, "I was in the Pease River fight, but I am not very proud of it. That was not a battle at all, but just a killing of squaws."[4]

The other Texas Ranger who left an extant account was Benjamin C. Dragoo. Dragoo also joined Ross's command on October 3, 1860, and received his discharge on February 5, 1861. His pay, like Rogers's compensation, totaled $102.50. His first documented recounting of the Battle of Pease River appeared in the December 1923 edition of *Frontier Times*, which reprinted it in April 1929. Another version of Dragoo's recollections can be found in the *Junction Eagle* for December 22, 1927, and reprinted in *Frontier Times* in February 1928.[5]

The information in the *Frontier Times* articles does not speak well for Dragoo's credibility. The author of the 1929 article writes that Dragoo was born in Washington County, Illinois, December 9, 1835, and when he was three years old he moved to Red River County, Texas, where he lived for one year. Then he writes, "Mr Dragoo says that when a small boy, he often played with Cynthia Ann Parker and lived only eight miles away when the Indians attacked [Parker's Fort and carried] Cynthia Ann into captivity."[6] But Parker was living in what is now Limestone County, Texas, on May 19, 1836, the date of her first capture. Even as the crow flies, the distance is considerably over one hundred miles from Red River County, and of course she was captured, and therefore unable to play with little one-year-old Ben Dragoo, two years before he had moved from Illinois. The childhood playmate statement prompted Araminta McClellan Taulman to make the comments that appear in chapter 1 about numerous errors in writings on Parker.

One might hope the author of the *Frontier Times* article had misunderstood Dragoo. Such hope, however, suffers when Dragoo, in his account printed in 1923, says, "Some . . . have stated that Quanah Parker was not there at the time of the fight. This is a mistake. He was present and shot away all his arrows and wounded two or three of our men. When . . . the boy had nothing left in his quiver, Frank Cassidy . . . rode up to where Quanah was crouching, patted his horse on the hip, and motioned the lad to mount up behind him, which the boy did without any hesitation, and from that day to this Quanah Parker has been the white man's friend."[7]

Clearly, Dragoo misspoke. Not a man in Sul Ross's command was wounded. Quanah was not present, was not captured, and was not the white man's friend until many years later. Dragoo also says, "A portion of the Indian encampment was along the bank of the narrow, shallow river next to us when the charge began. The Indians in this quarter made a break for the opposite side. Just below I saw several mounted Indians make it across where the bed of the stream was dry and hard." He further notes, "I rushed in among these [Indians], shooting right and left, and when I had reached some distance, say forty or fifty yards on

Ben Dragoo, ca. 1895. Reprinted by permission of
Texas Ranger Hall of Fame and Museum, Waco.

the other side, I dashed alongside an Indian woman . . . mounted and carrying a babe in her arms. I was just in the act of shooting her when, with one arm, she held up her baby and said 'Americano!' I then told her," he concluded, "to dismount and go back but seeing she did not understand me, I motioned her to the rear and left her."

Dragoo says he was the first to notice the captured woman was a white person, and he thought he had seen her somewhere in the past. He then claims to have told Ross, "Captain, I believe that woman is Cynthia Ann Parker." Almost immediately, Dragoo alleges, Parker said in a strong, clear voice: "Me Cynthia Ann."

Dragoo also talked about Ross's encounter with the chief. He states Ross had a fight at close quarters with a chief, and it "happened right in the village." During the scrap with the Indian leader, he says, the chief wounded Ross, whereupon Ross told his Mexican servant to shoot the man. The servant shot the Indian through the hips. Dragoo said, "This brought the chief to a sitting posture and while making the most horrid faces and defying his conquerors by grimace, and every other taunting gesture known to [Indians], one of the Rangers . . . ran up and knocked him on the head with his gun. With his knife, and while the chief was still kicking, he made a quick incision around his head from ear to ear, and when he jerked off his scalp it popped like a rifle." As to the death song tale, the wild, weird song Ross mentions, Dragoo states, "If that chief sang a death song that day it was after we left him—dead." Before he ends his account by describing the capture of forty-eight U.S. Army mules and some forty or fifty horses, Dragoo states, "Peter Robertson, of Cureton's company, [and I] were the advance scouts and trailers."[8]

All things considered, Dragoo's account of the battle is as credible as that of any other of those who claimed to be participants. His name appears on the Texas Ranger muster roll and, as will be seen, Peter Robertson mentions his presence at the battle. Of course, one should wonder about the accuracy of his story.

### Reports of the Citizen Militiamen

Among Captain Jack Cureton's citizen militia four men provided extant accounts. They include Peter Robertson, Jonathan Hamilton Baker, Francis Marion Peveler, and the future Texas Panhandle cattleman Charles Goodnight. Cureton's report, if he made one, has not been found.

Peter Robertson, like Texas Ranger Ben Dragoo, claimed he was acting as one of the principal scouts for the entire expedition. As a result, he said, he rode with the lead scout, Mr. Stewart, and not with the main body of Cureton's men. The scouting activities, he stated in 1920 or 1921, put him in the fight. "When we made the charge," he says, "most of the Indians had mounted, as if on the move and were taking an early start. We took them by surprise and they didn't have much show for a fight. When we dashed up to the tepees, firing at every Indian in sight, a [woman] who was already mounted, turned her horse facing us, and holding up a baby, hollered out, 'Americana!'" The chief, Peta Nocona, Robertson said, rallied his men and attempted a defense. "Seeing his efforts, Ross charged him," Robertson noted, "and it was then the hand-to-hand fight with the chief came off. I didn't see much of this fight between Ross and Old Peta, as just at that time I was mighty busy."

Robertson continued, "When Ross dashed on him he was using his six-shooter, while the Indian tried to unhorse him with his lance. Ross killed the chief's horse, and when the animal fell the Indian threw his lance at Ross . . . which struck [Ross's] horse's tail and this made the steed so ungovernable that Ross had to dismount." Then Ross with his last pistol shot broke the chief's arm. Ross "then drew his sword and advanced on the infuriated [Comanche], who, with his shield," said Robertson, "warded off the cuts and thrusts. At this stage of the game, some of the boys fired on the Indian and killed him, and as he went down he struck his head against a cottonwood tree that stood near on the bank of the creek." Robertson also noted, "The man who shot the Indian was some fifty or seventy-five yards away when he fired, and I afterwards heard Ross say to him, 'You made a splendid shot.'"[9]

Peter Robertson further stated: "Through the Mexican interpreter Cynthia Ann told us that she had three sons and the eldest, which afterwards proved to be Quanah, was about 16 years old, was then with a party on a raid down in the settlements. She cried a great deal while she was with us, and from what the Mexican said, she did not seem to grieve so much over the death of Peta Nocona, her husband, but believed that her two younger sons had been killed in the fight." Robertson also noted that twenty federal cavalrymen made up one arm of the expedition and that they and the Texas Rangers killed eighteen Comanches in a twenty-minute fight. He also mentioned that Ben Dragoo was involved in the fight.[10]

Robertson's account differs from the reports of the Texas Rangers, but not by much. Such differences include the death of the chief's horse, Ross's advancing on the chief with his sword drawn, several men's firing on the chief, and the eighteen dead Comanches. Robertson's published account first appeared about sixty years after the battle. He was, of course, a member of the expedition, but one can only guess whether he saw all that he reported.

Jonathan Hamilton Baker was also there. A Palo Pinto schoolteacher when he joined Jack Cureton's company, Baker kept a diary in which he made entries covering the entire period of the expedition to Pease River. Because he was with Cureton's company, he was not present for the fight but arrived on the scene sometime after it was over. As he did not witness the battle, he did not write about it in his diary. Nonetheless, his description of the battlefield is the best and most reliable one available. At least such is the case if one reads and relies on his original diary. Many people do not. The original diary is in the Tarrant County

Historical Commission's collection, and it consists of several boxes of both tablets and loose papers on which the diary is handwritten.[11]

There is also a typed document alleged to be a copy of the original. The copy is in the collections of the Dolph Briscoe Center for American History at the University of Texas at Austin. Baker's daughter, Elizabeth Baker, seems to have typed the document. In various places she inserted comments, thus indicating she prepared the typed version. It is not a complete copy of the original diary. Although the greater part of the document Elizabeth prepared is similar to the corresponding entries in the original diary, some notable additions exist, especially for the Battle of Pease River.[12]

A great many omissions exist as well. Consider, for example, the entries from March 1, 1858, when Baker began his diary, to October 27, 1861. For that period the copy typed by his daughter contains 123 pages with an average of 54 lines per page and an average of 73 characters and spaces per line. A modern typed copy of the original Tarrant County diary contains for the same period 185 pages with an average of 56 lines per page and an average of 103 characters and spaces per line. Obviously, the alleged copy in Austin is not an accurate transcription of the original diary.

Both the original and the copy contain many of the same entries. In the original diary, for Wednesday, December 19, Baker wrote: "We were off at 9 this morning. . . . Ross was off some time before us. We traveled up the river 10 or 12 miles and crossed the old trail that [comes] out from our country last. On this trail our guides found a pillow slip with a girl's belt and Mrs. Sherman's bible in it." He adds several revealing sentences: "They also found a fresh trail of five Indians that had just passed up the river. . . . As we were moving up the river on the trail . . . we saw Ross and company coming down the river on the opposite side meeting us. We were soon together and he informed us that he had overtaken a party of 15 Indians and had killed 12 of them and taken three prisoners."

Baker summed up the feelings of the militiamen and reviewed the battle results: "There was great ado, yelling, whooping, and hollering! . . . Our boys could not be restrained but charged eagerly to the scene of action. I was among them. We found only four dead Indians, all [women]. There were many packs strown [sic] on the prairie two or three miles with a large amount of beef, buffalo skins, camp accouterments &c &c." He noted that the "boys gathered up a large amount of tricks of various kinds . . . meat, . . . leather bags filled with marrow out of bones and branes [sic], little sacks of soup, sausages, the gut stuffed with tallow and branes [sic]. . . . We returned to the river . . . and found that they had taken about thirty horses and mules." Baker concluded, "The prisoners are a woman, a small child, and a boy about ten years old. . . . Our men are dissatisfied to some extent that Ross done all the fighting, and that we were left entirely out of the fight. Ross' men and the Regulars take the horses to themselves. Capt. Ross and Sergt. Spangler came to our camp and had a consultation with our officers."

For the next day, Thursday, December 20, 1860, Baker wrote: "Ross and the Dragoons left us for home this morning. . . . The boys are coming in this evening from the battle ground with meat." Later that day he noted, "Some of the men who came in late say that they trailed six or eight Indians who made their escape during the fight yesterday. So Capt. Ross was mistaken about killing all the Indians." He explained, "I think probably he was honestly mistaken, being deceived by the report of Sergt. Spangler of the Dragoons, who reported to him that he had killed a party of seven that ran in a different direction from where Ross was engaged." Then, Baker concluded, "We cannot find but one [Comanche] in this place killed, but we find the trail of six leaving this place, hence we legitimately conclude that Spangler lied and let his Indians get away. We can not find but seven Indians killed, four [women] and three [men]."[13]

The typewritten, alleged copy of the diary has interesting additions as to what took place during the battle and about activities afterward on the night of December 19. As has been noted, Baker was not at the fight, but in the typewritten copy at the Dolph Briscoe Center for American History someone added the following to Baker's handwritten December 19 entry: "When the soldiers came upon them, the [Indian men who] were left jumped on their horses and made after the main group. When the [Indian women] attempted to get on the horses with them the [men] pushed them off and rode away."

Also in the added entry is a discussion of the captured woman's identity. It reads: "Tonight as we sat about the campfire, a discussion arose as to [the woman's] identity, and in the course of the talk, some-one remarked that years ago a family by the name of Parker had been killed where Parker is now, and a child, Cynthia Ann Parker had been carried off. At once the woman spoke up and said, 'Me Cynthia Ann.'" The entry continues: "So we have decided that the long lost Cynthia Ann Parker has been recaptured."

Then came the addition of an apocryphal but romantic moccasin story: "As we sat about the camp fire I [Baker] picked up a tiny mocca-sin, and after looking at [it] decided to keep it as it was a beautiful one." But, on "glancing round I noticed the woman looking at me intently. I looked at her and the little child, and noticed it had on only one moc-casin, so I held up the one I had picked up, she nodded her head, and I held it out and the child came over and got it and the mother put it [on] for her."[14]

The report of men pushing women from their horses, the identity discussion, and the moccasin story, all part of the typed copy, are not in the original, handwritten Jonathan Baker diary in Tarrant County. The typed copy also presents problems related to its authenticity. First, for example, in his original, handwritten entries in which he mentions the federal troops from Camp Cooper, as he does in entries for December 9, 13, and 19, Baker refers to them as "Dragoons" or "Regulars," not as "soldiers," as in the typewritten addition.

Second, there is a problem of logic in the typed diary copy. Several Comanche women were afoot, or so the entry states, and, if the entry is authentic, the women must have made their escape or been killed, for the Americans captured only Parker and the two children. As Baker found only four dead women, what happened to the others? Again, if they were afoot, as the entry states, surely a mounted Texas Ranger or a cavalryman on horseback could have run down and captured a running woman.

And, third, there is the obviously fabricated campfire scene. Cynthia Ann Parker and her little girl were the prisoners of the Texas Rangers and federal troopers. They were in the Rangers' and troopers' encampment of about sixty men, which stood some distance from where Baker and the rest of Jack Cureton's company, seventy or more men, camped. Probably several fires, around each of which about a dozen men sat, existed in each bivouac. Baker wrote that Ross and Spangler came to Cureton's camp and had a consultation that night, the nineteenth. But the typewritten diary addition with the campfire story would have one believe Cureton's men, or some of them, were sitting around a fire with Parker and her little girl. Baker was sitting close enough to the woman and her child that they could see each other. It further indicates that Parker allowed the little girl to walk over to Baker to retrieve her moccasin.

Careful analysis suggests that the scenarios presented here, each from the typewritten version of the diary, do not fit descriptions of the battle in accounts of the other participants. Of course Baker was not present during the fight, and he did not see what is described in the

CYNTHIA ANN PARKER.

Cynthia Ann Parker with Prairie Flower, ca. 1861. Reprinted by
permission of Southwest Collection/Special Collections
Library, Texas Tech University, Lubbock.

fight portion of the typewritten copy of the diary. In addition, other sources, as well as sound logic, suggest Parker was not definitely identified and did not say "Me Cynthia Ann" until a few weeks later. While she was with the federal troops at Camp Cooper, her uncle Isaac Parker arrived and interviewed his niece. When he stated that his brother and his wife called her Cynthia Ann, she then indicated her name.

Despite the obviously flawed, or faked, additions in the typewritten version, some authors have included portions of it in their books or articles. Such inclusions are regrettable, for Baker's handwritten diary, the one in Tarrant County, contains probably the most reliable descriptions of the scene of the Battle of Pease River and the number of Indian casualties. The moccasin story as described in the typewritten diary, on the other hand, stretches one's confidence in the truth. When such obviously fictionalized additions are passed off as authentic diary entries, the daughter's typed copy of the diary loses credibility, but there is another version of the moccasin incident.

A third citizen militiaman who reported on the battle was Francis Marion Peveler. Born April 10, 1843, in Fannin County, Peveler moved with his family to Parker County, then to Palo Pinto County, and finally to Young County. While living in Young County, he joined Jack Cureton's company. Of course, as a member of Cureton's command, Peveler, like Baker, did not participate in or witness the fight. But not having participated in the Battle of Pease River did not keep some of the men who had arrived on the scene after the fight from describing the event, sometimes in great detail.[15]

On October 14, 1932, when he was eighty-nine years old, Peveler wrote some notes concerning some of his experiences and gave them to J. Evetts Haley, a Texas Panhandle and West Texas historian. The notes are transcribed in Peveler's handwriting, and parts of them are extremely difficult to read. Peveler writes that Sergeant John Spangler brought forty dragoons. He says also Cureton's men heard the gunfire from the battle but did not get to the battle scene until the fight was over. His notes, where they are legible, include the following: "Cynthia Ann sat [illegible] fire that [illegible], and had a little girl and was very playful. Boys had picked up one [Peveler had written "couple of" but he marked it out and substituted "one"] moccasin on battlefield. Little child saw it [and] ran [and] got it from the boy that had it and put it on. She was very [illegible] little girl."[16]

A narrative of Peveler's version of what happened at Pease River is published in G. A. Holland's *History of Parker County and the Double Log Cabin*. It follows Ross's authorized account, at least until the capture of Cynthia Ann Parker. In this version, Peveler describes the chase that Sul Ross narrated in his long account cited near the beginning of this chapter. Lieutenant Kelliher, he wrote, "followed on a long chase what he thought to be an Indian. When he caught up, ready to shoot, he saw what appeared to be a [woman], with a papoose strapped to her back. The Lieutenant was too brave a man to shoot a woman, even if [an Indian woman], and especially one with a child on her back." Peveler concluded, Kelliher "pressed close up beside them as they ran, caught the bridle rein and slowed them up. When no further resistance was offered he led them back to the commander."[17]

Peveler's report on the capture of Parker differs somewhat from Ross's account. Sul Ross stated that both he and Kelliher rode up to Parker's horse, and Ross was about to shoot when she held up her child. Peveler writes that Kelliher was about to do the shooting, and he does not mention Ross as being there. Peveler also claims the child was strapped to Parker's back; he does not mention her holding the child up. Of course Peveler did not see the events, as he was not there. He does not say where he got his information, nor for that matter does he suggest why anyone would even bother to ask him to write his account of something he did not see or in which he did not participate.

One should note again the moccasin story. Francis Peveler, like Jonathan Baker, was part of Cureton's command. Thus, neither of them would have been around a campfire with Parker. Note also that in the typed copy of Baker's diary, it is claimed he picked up the moccasin as he sat around the campfire, but Peveler claimed it was picked up on the battlefield.[18]

No one may ever know where Peveler acquired his version. During the later years of their lives, both Baker and Peveler lived in or near Granbury, Texas. Baker predeceased Peveler by several years. Whether they got together during their lifetimes or whether family members got together after Baker's death we will never know.

And then, for whatever reasons, Peveler claimed Albert Sidney Johnston was the commanding officer at Camp Cooper when Parker arrived there as a captive. Post returns, however, show Captain Nathan G. Evans as the commanding officer at Camp Cooper for the entire month of December 1860 and for at least the first three weeks of January 1861, when Captain Stephen D. Carpenter relieved him of command. Johnston was not at Camp Cooper at that time, nor was he in Texas. On December 21, 1860, Johnston left New York on a ship bound for California via Panama. He arrived in California about the middle of January 1861.[19]

Also among Cureton's command was Charles Goodnight. Born March 5, 1836, Goodnight was about twenty-four years old when he participated in the Pease River expedition. Later in life he talked at some length about it, and on November 13, 1926, he dictated to J. Evetts Haley what he called "My Recollections and Memories of the Capture of Cynthia Ann Parker."[20]

To paraphrase, Goodnight said that Sul Ross had raised a company of twenty-five Texas Rangers. Captain J. J. Cureton had raised a company of twenty-five men and joined Ross at Belknap. The commander at Camp Cooper sent Ross twenty-five troopers. They all got together at Belknap. One of the leaders asked Goodnight to serve as scout and guide of the expedition, a position he kept as long as he was in the service. While on the march, the Texas Rangers and federal troopers camped in one area and Cureton's militiamen camped in another. The Rangers and troopers with Goodnight got off ahead of Cureton's men. Later Goodnight noticed a Bible lying in the grass on the trail. It belonged to Mrs. Sherman. He noticed some trees about a quarter of a mile distant and he went to investigate. Upon arriving at the trees, he discovered "sign" that an Indian party had just left.

Goodnight then decided the Indian camp was probably near some fresh water about one and one-half miles to the west. He rode out in view of Cureton's men and gave the signal to charge, which they did "pell mell." Ross, who was ahead of Goodnight and Cureton, had already ordered his company to charge the Indian camp. The Rangers passed through the Indian women and shot the men as they came to them. The troopers killed all the women. Ross had a hand-to-hand fight with the chief and killed him. Cynthia Ann Parker was carrying a little girl about three or four months old. A little boy was riding double behind the chief and the chief pushed him off the horse. Ross picked the boy up and placed him behind him on his horse. Cureton's men were not in the fight but in plain view and a very short distance from the scene of the action. Cureton sent Goodnight to look for signs indicating some Comanches may have escaped. Goodnight found the trail of two Indians who had fled. Ross thought he had killed Peta Nocona, a chief. Peta Nocona was never a chief and was not there at the time of the fight, but had left two days before with his two boys, Quanah and Peanut.[21]

Goodnight's recollections occur in four places: in manuscript form at the Panhandle Plains Historical Museum, in a pamphlet published in 1926, in an article J. Evetts Haley edited and published in the *Panhandle-Plains Historical Review* in 1928, and in Haley's 1935 biography of Goodnight. The published recollections in the 1928 article are in many ways identical with Goodnight's 1926 recollections and the pamphlet. In the 1928 version, Ross still had twenty-five Rangers and twenty-five

Charles Goodnight, ca. 1900. Reprinted by permission of Southwest
Collection/Special Collections Library, Texas Tech University, Lubbock.

troopers from Camp Cooper, but now Cureton's command had increased to eighty men. Also, Goodnight stated in 1928, when Cureton and six or eight of his men topped the sand hills, the men were in plain sight of the ensuing battle but took no part in it. He recalled the fight as lasting only a few minutes, and no Texas Ranger shot a woman. Not only did the chief push the boy from the back of his horse but also other Comanche men pushed children off their horses. He recalled seeing Cynthia Ann Parker's hands as extremely dirty on account of handling a lot of meat. Goodnight believed he was the first to notice that Parker, whose grief was intense and distressing, was not a Comanche. According to Goodnight the command had a Mexican acting as a very poor interpreter. The interpreter, said Goodnight, knew no Comanche and Parker knew no English or Spanish.[22]

The name of the chief Ross killed was Nobah, or so Goodnight claimed, and Goodnight got the information from old Comanche warriors. He also indicated that during the winter of 1877 and 1878 Quanah Parker, who was on Goodnight's Palo Duro Canyon ranch at the time, gave him the same information.[23]

Goodnight's accounts present several problems. He was not the scout for the expedition. A Mr. Stewart acted as Ross's scout and guide. If he served as a scout for anyone, Goodnight guided Cureton's command, which needed a scout only because of the growing distance that separated it from the federal troops and Ross's Texas Rangers. That Goodnight was in fact the scout for Cureton's command is confirmed by Goodnight's claim that it was he who found Mrs. Sherman's Bible and by Baker's December 19 diary entry, which stated, "On this trail our guides found a pillow slip with a girl's belt and Mrs. Sherman's bible in it." The militiamen's poor mounts caused them to drop behind the others, and as a result Cureton probably found conditions increasingly difficult for following the trail without a scout. Goodnight admits the Ross and Spangler commands were ahead of him even when he was scouting.

Goodnight, like so many others remotely connected to the battle, was anxious to embellish his participation. For reasons known only to him, he had the numbers of Texas Rangers, federal cavalry troops, and, at least in one account, Cureton's men wrong. He claims that he gave the signal for Cureton's men to charge, and they did, as he says, "pell mell." If Goodnight is correct about the charge, why did Jonathan Baker write in his diary on the day of the fight that Ross and his men going downstream met Cureton's command coming upriver and at the meeting told the militiamen about the fight? Why did Hiram Rogers say it took Cureton's men four hours to get to the scene of the fight?

Because there were only seven Comanches killed in the fight, Goodnight's claim about who killed the women needs close review. Recall that according to Jonathan Baker, the most reliable authority on the battleground scene and consequently the number of Indians killed, Cureton's men after two days of searching were able to find the bodies of only seven Comanches: four women, all of whom were found the first day, and three men. On the second day Cureton's men found the body of an Indian who had been killed by the federal troops. The person must have been a male, as the total number of women killed never rose above the initial four found the previous day.

If Goodnight's claim that the Texas Rangers killed only men and federal troops killed the women were correct (which it is not), then the supposed twenty Rangers and Ross killed two Indians. As one of the two was the alleged chief Ross killed without the aid of any other Ranger, the other twenty or so Rangers must have been able to kill only one Indian.

In his official report to Governor Sam Houston, Ross stated that he gave a pistol to C. R. Gray, the first Ranger to kill an Indian. Consequently, according to Goodnight, Gray was the only Ranger other than Ross to have killed an Indian at Pease River, hardly a glorious military accomplishment for the Rangers. It would, of course, have made Ross's decision as to whom to give the pistol quite easy. Because in Texas mythology the Rangers have always enjoyed a reputation for outstanding marksmanship, perhaps Goodnight should have joined Ranger Hiram Rogers in admitting that the Rangers killed women during the Pease River fight.[24]

Even Sul Ross himself claimed he killed a young girl. Ross said he did not know she was a girl, and he is probably correct. It would be difficult to determine the sex of a rider who was bundled in winter clothing and buffalo robes for protection from the cold north wind. Perhaps because he did not want anyone to think a Texas Ranger would kill a female, even by accident, Goodnight substituted a boy for the girl riding behind the chief and had the chief throw him off rather than have Ross shoot him. But perhaps not.[25]

If his recollections are correct, what happened to the other children Goodnight saw thrown off their horses? Were they among the seven killed? Were the children afoot able to escape the mounted Rangers? If Goodnight was close enough to see all the action he reports, why did he not get in the battle? How much of what he describes could he have witnessed? The answer is that Goodnight in actuality was back with Cureton's men, all of whom, except Peter Robertson, because of the poor condition of their horses, were working their way up the Pease River and did not participate in the attack.

The truth perhaps is that Charles Goodnight, like many of the men whose stories about their adventures along Mule Creek are recorded, attempted to place himself and his friends in as significant positions as possible. Sometimes such efforts meant constructing a bit of information about incidents that did not occur. Sometimes it meant claiming to have participated in events in which the informants had little or no role.

In summary, of the four members of Cureton's company whose accounts are extant, only one, Peter Robertson, was probably involved in the battle. Jonathan Baker admits he was not in the fight but arrived on the scene afterward. Goodnight claims to have witnessed the fight and to have given the signal for a charge into the Indians' camp. He also claims to have seen much of the battle close up, but for some reason he was unable to get involved in the fight itself. Peveler does not claim to have been in the fight, as he states that "they," not "we," charged the Indian camp. Consequently his description of the battle is nothing more than hearsay gathered either from participants or from books and articles. His account was not the only description of the fight derived solely from hearsay, but, as with similar narratives, it has received attention from those who write about the Battle of Pease River.

## Sergeant Spangler's Reports

Sergeant John W. Spangler was in command of twenty cavalrymen who participated in the Battle of Pease River. He had been in the 1858 fight at Wichita village with Sul Ross, and a year after the fight he received a wound during a fight along Small Creek, or Crooked Creek, in Kansas. He remained loyal to the Union during the Civil War, and on July 28, 1866, he received promotion to captain. He died September 17, 1867.

Sergeant Spangler twice reported on the Battle of Pease River. His two accounts and Ross's report to Governor Sam Houston, which will be discussed in chapter 3, represent the only "official" reports of the battle. The three "official" explanations appeared within a month of the battle and therefore should not suffer from anyone's faulty memory. Whether any of them suffer from prejudice, falsehoods, or related peccadilloes may be another matter.

Before making such judgment, one needs to consider all three reports. At the time, the winter of 1860–61, Texas and the entire nation swirled in political turmoil that soon led to the Civil War. Two days before the Battle of Pease River, Governor Sam Houston issued a proclamation to convene a special session of the Texas legislature for January 21, 1861. Its members were to consider the state's political connection with the federal government and the idea of secession. One day after the battle, South Carolina seceded from the Union. By the time Sergeant Spangler wrote his second report on January 16, Mississippi, Alabama, and Florida had seceded, with Georgia and Louisiana soon to follow. Before the end of the month delegates to the Texas secession convention also voted in favor of leaving the United States.

And on February 21, 1861, the idea of secession in Northwest Texas became real. On that fateful day probably many of the Texas Rangers and members of Jack Cureton's militia company who had ridden with U.S. cavalrymen on the Pease River expedition made up a contingent of Texans who demanded the surrender of Camp Cooper from federal troops. These were troubling times.

In the meantime, Spangler had sent his first report, dated December 24, 1860, just five days after the battle, to Captain Nathan G. Evans, commanding officer at Camp Cooper. To paraphrase, he said his detachment of twenty men joined Ross's Texas Rangers on December 11 along Elm Creek, and their combined force met about seventy citizens at the head of Salt Creek. After several days of travel, his report notes, they saw a group of about twenty-five Comanches, whom they charged and overtook. In a hotly contested battle of about thirty minutes, they killed fourteen Indians and took three prisoners. They also captured forty-five animals. Some of the Comanches escaped because of the exhausted condition of the pursuers' horses, which for several days had scarcely anything to eat but cottonwood limbs. Spangler noted he had the assistance of Captain Ross, Lieutenants Tom Kelliher and David Sublett, and about ten other Rangers. The remaining Rangers were not there because of the poor condition of their horses. He ended his report by noting the federal troopers used only their revolvers during the engagement.[26]

Circumstances surrounding Spangler's second report are intriguing. On February 2, 1861, about six weeks after the battle, the *San Antonio Ledger and Texan* printed a letter Captain Evans of Camp Cooper had written on January 17, 1861, to Major W. A. Nichols, Assistant Adjutant General, Department of Texas. In the letter Evans wrote, "Agreeable to the instructions of your official letter on 10th inst, I have the honor to report the result of my inquiry of Sergeant Spangler, relative to the part the State troops took in the engagement on the 19th of December last, with the hostile Comanches on Pease river." Undoubtedly Nichols had inquired about getting a more thorough accounting from Sergeant Spangler, the ranking federal officer at Mule Creek. Thus, on January 16 Spangler handed a report to Evans, who then enclosed it with his letter to Nichols.[27] Copies of the January 10, 1861, Nichols request, the January 17 Evans letter, and Spangler's second report, dated January 16, cannot be located in the National Archives. Consequently, the letter and report printed in the *San Antonio Ledger* are all that remain available.

According to Captain Evans's letter, Major Nichols must have been curious about the part the Texas Rangers played in the Battle of Pease River. Why was this so? What had Nichols heard or read that would cause him to seek more detailed information about the Rangers' participation? Because his letter is not available, we may never know what triggered Nichols's curiosity. One possible reason might be the battle narrative Captain Sul Ross filed with Governor Sam Houston. Ross wrote his "official" version of the battle on January 4, 1861, in Waco. In it, and in his authorized account, Ross stated he sent Cynthia Ann Parker to Camp Cooper, and he went to Waco to meet Governor Houston. There is a possibility Ross gave his January 4 report personally to Houston at the meeting. Later, in Austin, Nichols may have seen it. Ross's "official" report contains an instructive sentence that may have piqued Major Nichols's interest and led to his inquiry: "As for the three men of the Second Cavalry who were with me, it is enough to say that they were of H Company, and under Sergeant Spangler."[28] Was Ross claiming there were only three men of the Second Cavalry with him? If so, why in his authorized account did he claim all twenty of the federal troops participated in the attack? Of course, Major Nichols would have been familiar with Sergeant Spangler's December 24, 1860, report wherein Spangler wrote that twenty of his men and only about thirteen Texas Rangers participated in the fight. If he had seen a copy of the Ross report to Governor Houston, Nichols would have had very good reason to request additional information concerning Ranger participation in the battle. Such, of course, is speculation, and there may have been other reasons for Nichols's inquiry.

In response to Major Nichols's request, Captain Evans, as noted, obtained the second report from Sergeant Spangler. In it, Spangler said the cavalry was under his command, meaning, of course, Sul Ross was not in command of the cavalry, as claimed by some people. Also in the report, dated January 16, 1861, Spangler says Ross's men were "indifferently mounted, the greater portion being mounted on small horses and in very poor condition. My instructions were to cooperate with Capt. Ross, but his movements being so slow, my men began to lose all patience and hopes of seeing the Indians."

Then he wrote,

> I told Capt. Ross that I would charge the main body of Indians on the right while he would charge on the left. When the command was given to charge my men were all in advance of the State troops, in fact I did not see more than 5 or 6 of them at the time the charge was made, but in justice to Capt. Ross and his men I beg here to state, that after the

fight was over, upon inspection, I found 3 dead Indians on the side of the ravine where he had been engaged, whilst on the portion of the battle field where the cavalry had been engaged, I found 11.

He claimed that "at no time during the engagement were the cavalry and State troops near each other, as they were separated by a deep ravine." He confirmed that "Ross took one small boy as prisoner, and I took two prisoners in the engagement." Sergeant Spangler concluded his long report by writing that Dr. S. L. Nidelett, who was the Texas Ranger surgeon at Pease River, "was an eyewitness of the charge throughout, and remarked had Capt. Ross' men been engaged where the cavalry were, they would have all been killed, for what few he had in the fight no two were together."[29]

A quick review of the reports, reminiscences, and interviews of several members of the Pease River expedition reveals discrepancies and likely some fabrications. If memory is constructed, as David Thelen argues, plenty of creative nonfiction exists in the reporting of the massacre along Mule Creek. The eyewitness accounts as presented in this chapter provided the ingredients for later writers to fashion stories consistent with a collective memory, but a corrupted memory, that created a mythic Texas history and Texas mystique inconsistent with a new, more inclusive and usable past.

# 3
## THE REPORTS
## Lawrence Sullivan Ross

O ver a span of thirty-odd years Texas Ranger captain Sul Ross put forward his several accounts of the enigmatic episode along Mule Creek not far from where it joins the Pease River. While they may not have understood the term "collective memory," Ross and his political friends, by the ways in which they revised Ross's accounts, seemed to have grasped the idea of constructing historical memories. Consciously or not, to paraphrase historian Gregg Cantrell about a related matter, they sought to instill in Texans of the late nineteenth century a particular memory of the state's history that would serve their needs. Over the years Ross told, wrote, rewrote, and embellished his descriptions of the Battle of Pease River and the 1860 capture of Cynthia Ann Parker and by doing so altered public perceptions of the paired events.[1]

As a result of his shifting accounts, Sul Ross became the principal beneficiary of the bloody massacre reinvented as the Battle of Pease River. Cynthia Ann Parker (Naudah) gained nothing from the retelling or from the battle and her capture. Neither did her husband, Peta Nocona, or their two sons, Quanah and Pecos, and least of all her infant daughter. Truth be told, the family suffered immeasurably from her 1860 capture. The event brought grief and despair to most of the Comanches involved but benefited Ross in dramatic ways. In fact, a contemporary of Ross claimed it was "this Pease River fight and the capture of Cynthia Ann Parker that made Sul Ross governor of Texas."[2]

Ross entered politics in the 1870s. He became sheriff of McLennan County in 1873 and served as a member of the Constitutional Convention of 1876. In 1880 he won election as a state senator. As a politician, Ross became aware of the political benefit of the increasingly famous battle and the 1860 capture of Parker. Thus, he encouraged friends and supporters to produce campaign literature, especially sketches of his military exploits, that mentioned not only his Civil War experience but also the Pease River fight and his important role in it. Over the years the story grew more elaborate.

Ross gave several accounts of the battle. The most often cited description, quoted in full in chapter 2, is the one that became the authorized account. It first appeared in James T. DeShields's book *Cynthia Ann Parker*. In the preface the author states that in writing the book he used information furnished him by Victor M. Rose, Major John Henry Brown, and Sul Ross, among others, and that his book was a "narrative of plain, unvarnished facts."[3]

Of the people mentioned in DeShields's preface, only Ross participated in the Pease River fight and the capture of Parker. Consequently, DeShields's account of both the battle and the capture must have come from Ross, either directly or indirectly, for the others were not present at Mule Creek.

What did DeShields mean when he wrote that his book contained "plain, unvarnished facts"? He noted, for example, that the battle was

Lawrence Sullivan "Sul" Ross during the Civil War, ca. 1863.
Courtesy of Texas Collection, Baylor University, Waco, Texas.

fought between a superior force of Comanches and sixty Texas Rangers. But only about fifteen Indians were in the camp, and no more than twenty Rangers and twenty federal troops attacked the village. Assuming DeShields was using the word "superior" to refer to numbers and not some character trait, the Rangers and federal troops, not the Comanches, had the decidedly superior fighting force, especially since the majority of the Indians were probably unarmed women.

DeShields "varnished" his facts further when he claimed, "So signal a victory had never before been gained over the fierce and war-like Comanches." The Comanches, although saddened by their loss, would have been delighted had the December 1860 loss of four women and three men in a battle against about forty Texas Rangers and federal troops been their most notable defeat. During the decade of the 1850s the Comanches received a number of devastating blows, including villages destroyed and people led away. They saw their range of territory cut in size and sliced through with trails that constantly grew larger, disrupting bison herds and bringing Anglos through their homeland. They saw bison numbers decrease and their own population decline. Without question, DeShields got this part of the story wrong.

DeShields continues his embellishments: "[Never] since that fatal December day in 1860 have [the Comanches] made any military demonstrations at all commensurate with the fame of their proud campaigns in the past. The great Comanche confederacy was forever broken. The incessant and sanguinary war which had been waged for more than thirty years was now virtually at an end. The blow was a most decisive one, as sudden and irresistible as a thunderbolt, and as remorseless and crushing as the hand of Fate."[4]

Numerous devastating Comanche and Kiowa raids occurred during the Civil War and afterward until about the time of the Red River War in 1874–75. DeShields's reasons for such hyperbole are known only to him, but the embellishments and fabrications would certainly sell books. All the Texas Ranger participants in the battle, their families, and Ross's political supporters might well purchase a book that described their own, their kinsman's, or Ross's deeds in such favorable and heroic light.

The exact year DeShields got this narrative from Ross is difficult to ascertain. DeShields's preface is dated May 19, 1886, and therefore it was probably before 1886 when he got Ross's story. What makes the year even more difficult to determine is the fact that DeShields quotes Ross as claiming that Pease Ross, the Indian boy captured in the battle, "died in McLennan County last year."[5] That statement places the boy's death in 1885 or earlier. In an unpublished manuscript in the Ross Family Papers in the Texas Collection at Baylor University, however, Ross is quoted as saying Pease Ross "died in McLennan County in 1887."[6] Because Ross likely would not tell DeShields the boy had died when in fact he was still alive, the 1887 date in the Ross Family Papers seems incorrect.

Moreover, in an article in the *Southwestern Historical Quarterly* in 1990, Lawrence T. Jones III claims Pease Ross, whom Jones describes as a respected citizen of McLennan County, died in 1883. Jones cites a footnote in Judith Ann Benner's *Sul Ross, Soldier, Statesman, Educator*, but the footnote does not give a death date for Pease Ross. Regardless of his source, if Jones is correct about 1883 being the year of the young man's death, then Ross gave his account to DeShields in 1884.[7]

The date is significant. If the 1887 date given in the Ross Family Papers is not a typographical error, Ross's narrative in the Ross Family Papers was made after 1887, and, consequently, the story given DeShields was the earlier account. And that is important. The Ross Family Papers provide a great deal of information about Ross's life, but concerning Ross's account of the Mule Creek fight and capture of

Parker the two narratives are almost identical, as if one were a copy of the other.

Which is the copy? Consider what is known. The Ross Family Papers account describes the Comanche hunting camp as "a large Comanche village," whereas DeShields describes it as simply a Comanche village. Both accounts state that during the Mule Creek fight, after Ross left Lieutenant Tom Kelliher with Parker, the Ranger captain continued pursuing the chief. The Ross Family Papers describe this event as follows: "I called to Lieut. Kelliheir [sic] to hold on to this captive as my hands were quite full in reckoning with this inveterate and powerful foe I was determined to conquer." In DeShields's authorized account Ross simply says, "I kept on after the chief."

Knowing how DeShields varnished and embellished his story, it is difficult to imagine his not mentioning the "large" Comanche village; after all, he stated that the Comanches were the superior force. Likewise, one wonders about DeShields's failure to describe the chief as an "inveterate and powerful foe."

In addition, the account in the Ross Family Papers contains a story of Ross's nearly shooting Cynthia Ann Parker. The tale has Ross saying, "Supposing her to be a man I was in the act of shooting her when she held up her child and stopped." In the DeShields book, Ross simply states, "I was in the act of shooting when she held up her child and stopped." Undoubtedly, someone thought that in the Ross Family Papers it should be made clear Ross would never intentionally shoot a woman. After all, when describing Ross's killing of the girl riding behind the chief, both accounts claim he thought she was a man. The fair conclusion, therefore, is that the story in the Ross Family Papers followed in time and substance the DeShields narrative, and it may have come much later.

Not all contemporaries were fans of DeShields's book and the authorized account. Dr. Morse Kent Taylor, post surgeon at Fort Sill in 1886–87, for example, had read *Cynthia Ann Parker*. He told Marion T. Brown, John Henry Brown's daughter, who from November 16, 1886, to February 19, 1887, was visiting Fort Sill, that he thought the author was "no writer at all."[8] To his credit, by the time he published *Border Wars of Texas* in 1912, DeShields, whose vocation was book agent, had reduced the number of Texas Rangers and federal cavalry troops involved in the battle from sixty to forty. Because he claims in *Cynthia Ann Parker* to be quoting Ross, DeShields in 1912 appears to be of the opinion that Ross had been either mistaken or untruthful when he said all forty of the Rangers were involved in the battle.[9]

The Ross account in DeShields's book remains significant, for as noted earlier, it is cited in many articles and books that touch on the Battle of Pease River and the 1860 capture of Cynthia Ann Parker. J. W. Wilbarger, in his 1889 book *Indian Depredations in Texas*, and Robert H. Williams, in his 1972 article "The Case for Peta Nocona," both cite DeShields and quote verbatim the Ross account as it appears in DeShields's book.[10]

Although the DeShields narrative of 1886 remains the standard, popular account, Ross gave other versions of the battle. The first person to record a Ross report of the battle was Jonathan Baker. In his diary entry for December 19, 1860, the day of the fight, Baker wrote that Ross informed Jack Cureton's men his command had "overtaken a party of 15 [Comanches] and had killed 12 of them and had taken three prisoners."[11]

A December 23, 1860, report to a correspondent of the *Dallas Herald* was the first Ross version of the Pease River fight to be published. It did not give details of a fight with an Indian chief or the capture of

Possibly Marion T. Brown, ca. 1898. Reprinted by permission of Brown Family Papers Collection, Dolph Briscoe Center for American History, University of Texas at Austin.

Parker. Ross told the correspondent there were thirteen Indian deaths, and the correspondent got the impression, or at least he reported, the entire party of Comanches had been killed or captured.[12]

Ross's next account is contained in the lost or stolen, at least missing, official report Ross sent to Governor Sam Houston. Several writers have mentioned that the Ranger captain filed no official report of the battle.[13] As early as 1935, for example, J. Evetts Haley in his book *Charles Goodnight: Cowman and Plainsman* wrote, "Unfortunately, there seems to be no contemporary report by Ross."[14]

But there is. In February 1908 the *San Antonio Express* and the *Beeville Bee* printed a letter E. M. Phelps, assistant adjutant general of Texas, wrote in response to a claim by Charles D. A. Loeffler, a retired U.S. Quartermaster Department officer, that he (Loeffler), while a member of the Second Cavalry in 1860, had captured Parker in the Battle of Pease River. Phelps states: "This claim on the part of Major Loaffler [*sic*], as shown by the original report of Capt. L. S. Ross, commanding [a] company [of] Texas Rangers, to Gov. Sam Houston, made on January 4, 1861, not quite two weeks after the fight, has no foundation. . . . In corroboration of the above a copy of the original report, now on file in the adjutant general's department, is printed."[15]

Below the introduction, both newspapers state that what follows is a "Copy of Gov. L. S. Ross' report to Gen. Sam Houston of an 'Indian fight' on Pease river, December 18, 1860, as taken from the original report on file in the adjutant general's office." The papers erred, of course, in stating that the battle was on December 18, 1860, and the apparent willingness of the paper's writer to accept the December 18 date remains a bit astonishing. The Ross report to Governor Houston, the very report the newspapers printed, states the battle was on December 19. The unquestioning acceptance of the wrong date may have been carelessness or may indicate that the writer did not bother to read the report he was printing. Or, if he did read it, perhaps he thought, since the report's date of December 19 differed from the one found in the authorized account, that the report must have had the incorrect date. Perhaps the writer was not familiar with the authorized account, and the date of December 18 was nothing more than a typographical error. If not, it is another example of how error is perpetuated in myth and the collective memory of Texans is affirmed.

The E. M. Phelps letter is revealing. It indicates that the "official," January 4, 1861, Ross report to Governor Sam Houston was on file in the adjutant general's office in February 1908. Houston himself writes about the report, telling legislative members on January 21, 1861, that they would see the Ross report shortly. It is difficult to tell from Houston's speech if he is waiting on the report from Ross or if Houston will present it to the legislature later, for he said the Comanches had been defeated "by a force under command of Captain Ross, whose report will be submitted."[16] Sometime between 1908 and 1935 the official Ross report disappeared from the adjutant general's office. It is still missing. Was it misplaced, removed, or stolen?

In his report to Governor Houston, Captain Ross makes several statements that are important in helping to understand exactly what happened during the Pease River fight and Parker's capture. In it, Ross states that a Mr. Stewart of Belknap served as the expedition's guide. He also writes that on December 19, 1860, Sergeant John Spangler of the Second Cavalry accompanied Ross on a ride to a "prominent peak" for observation. When they arrived at the position, the report notes, they found they were within two hundred yards of a Comanche village consisting of eight or nine grass tents, which the Indians, fifteen in number, were just deserting.

Essentially, the report states the following: Owing to the starved and jaded condition of their horses, not more than twenty of the Texas Rangers participated in the fight. By the time Ross had his men ready, the Indians had moved out on a level plain. The Comanches became aware of the Rangers and federal troops only when the enemy approached within two hundred yards. Consequently, many of the Indians died before they could make preparation for defense. Several, however, succeeded in getting about two miles from the village before the Rangers or troopers killed them. The surprise was so great that the Comanches could not shoot their arrows with much accuracy or precision, but they managed to wound Ross's horse and the mount of Private James Ireland. Twelve Indians died, and the son of the chief and a white woman and child were captured.

The Ross report continues: During the engagement Lieutenant Tom Kelliher saw an Indian mounted on a fleet pony, and he started in pursuit. After a chase of two miles, when he was just in the act of shooting, a white woman held up her baby and cried "Americano." Lieutenant David Sublett captured the son of the chief and took him up behind his saddle, but, seeing there were others endeavoring to make their escape, Sublett threw him off, and F. C. Donohoe afterwards took him up. Ross claims his men captured about forty head of animals, and he mentions only three men of the Second Cavalry as being with him. The report also contains the following statement: "Lieutenant [M. W.] Somerville came very near being killed by the chief, who had dismounted, evidently determined to sell his life as dearly as possible. Lieutenant Somerville endeavored to charge by him and shoot, but his horse made a short halt, when the Indian, too sure of his victim, let fly his arrow just as Lieutenant Somerville fell over on the opposite side of his horse."[17]

The official report to Governor Houston made no exaggerated claims. In it, as in his December 1860 report to the *Dallas Herald* correspondent, Ross gives the correct date of the battle as being December 19, and he makes no statement that a chief was killed and certainly no claim that he chased and killed a chief.

A bit over a decade later, Sul Ross erred on the date of the battle, a mistake he would continue to make in each of his subsequent accounts. The mistake, which gives the date of the battle as December 18, appeared in the early 1870s in a letter Ross addressed to one John Robinson and sent to the *Galveston News* for publication. The letter was not printed then, but some three or four years later it landed in the June 3, 1875, edition of the *News*, and two weeks later in the June 19 edition of the *Dallas Weekly Herald*.[18] No explanation for the long delay exists. This letter represents Ross's third published account of the fight, and he describes it as a "correct history" of the Pease River events. According to the letter, only twenty Texas Rangers participated in the battle, but Ross reports all twenty of the cavalry troopers joined the fight. The affair was over in less than thirty minutes, and the men killed or scattered 350 head of horses.

Further, in the letter Ross writes: "During the fight two Indians, well mounted, attempted to escape to the mountains, about six miles distance, and Lieutenant Tom [Kelliher], being well mounted, started in pursuit of one, and Lieutenant Somerville and myself after the other. Lieutenant S. being a heavy man, his horse soon failed and I had the chase to myself for two miles, when I came up with Mohee, the Comanche chief of that party of Indians, and after a short fight I killed him, and took possession of his shield, quiver, lance and head-dress, which are now with the archives in Austin." Ross then states:

> In a few minutes Lieutenant Tom [Kelliher] came back to where I was with an Indian [woman] and a young child in his [her?] arms. . . . After looking at her for the second time I told Tom he had captured a white woman. . . . On the way back to where the thickest of the fight had occurred I came upon a small Comanche boy who had been picked up, first by Lieutenant Sublett, and thrown down, and then by others, with the like result, and, fearing that he might eventually be killed by some of the more reckless men, I took him up behind me and carried him back to where I went into camp.

He concluded, "At the camp I called up a Mexican who had been raised by the Comanches and through him soon gained sufficient information of the woman to convince me that she had been captured in childhood. . . . Two of her sons by an Indian husband were killed in the battle."[19]

About ten years later, but at least by late 1885, Sul Ross had decided to run for governor of Texas. He won the subsequent election in 1886 and took office on January 18, 1887. During the election year, DeShields's book, *Cynthia Ann Parker*, appeared, and no doubt DeShields's exaggerated description of the battle, including Ross's authorized account, benefited the Ross campaign. The publication of the book and Ross's changed story were seemingly timed to coincide with his run for governor.

Indeed, a few years earlier, in October 1880, when he was a candidate for the Texas Senate, Ross had also attempted to use the Battle of Pease River for political gain. He sent a letter to his friend and journalist Victor M. Rose, the same Rose who provided DeShields a statement for use in *Cynthia Ann Parker*. At the time, 1880, Rose was in the process of compiling a sketch concerning some of Ross's exploits, including the capture of Parker. In the letter Sul Ross cautiously writes, "If the papers will not publish without marking it as advertised matter, I would rather you would withhold it. If however they place it in the Editorials or news from correspondents & there should be a charge made I would be ready to respond." In other words, Ross did not want the public to think it was printed for political purposes, but by 1880 he had determined some political advantage existed from his participation in the Pease River fight and the capture of Parker. He concluded the October 5, 1880, letter by writing, "I am satisfied the publication of this would swell my vote greatly."[20]

On April 21, 1881, Ross wrote again to Victor Rose concerning a biography of Ross. In the letter Ross states, "When dressed up for the public by your graceful pen it will make a book that will at least prove interesting to partial friends and <u>amuse the children</u>." Ross also writes, "I can only promise to supply you with the merest outlines by way of suggestions and trust the embellishment thereof to yourself."[21] The letters suggest that Sul Ross expected Rose and, for that matter, probably DeShields to embellish their accounts to improve his vote.

A look at the changes Ross made in his accounts may shed light on just how great a swell in his vote he thought the events would generate. As previously mentioned, his first two reports of the Pease River fight were his description to men of Cureton's company on the day of the battle and the account he gave, for publication, to a *Dallas Herald* correspondent on December 23, 1860. His official report to Governor Houston, written about two weeks after the battle, was more detailed. In that version of the battle, as well as in his next (the letter published in both the *Galveston News* and *Dallas Weekly Herald* in 1875), Ross states that, because of the poor condition of their horses, only twenty of his Texas Rangers were involved in the fight. But in the mid-1880s, in the DeShields authorized account, all forty of the Rangers were involved. Perhaps for political reasons Ross denied no Ranger the possible glory derived from the capture of Cynthia Ann Parker. Probably all of them were eligible voters.

In the 1861 report to Governor Houston, Ross notes there were about fifteen Indians in the village, a statement similar to the one he gave Cureton's men and the *Dallas Herald* correspondent in December 1860. By the 1870s, however, Ross was not reporting the number of Comanches. There is small glory in forty to sixty armed men attacking and killing thirteen or fifteen people, most of them women and children, especially when DeShields was telling everyone who read his book that the Comanches had the superior force. Why would Ross, who was seeking office, want to discredit DeShields's exaggerations when such falsehoods would benefit him politically? Indeed, he rather expected DeShields, like Rose before him, to embellish the story.

Of major significance is the account of the killing of the alleged chief. In his 1861 report to Houston, Ross identifies Lieutenant M. W. Somerville as the Texas Ranger nearly killed by a chief. The chief had purposely dismounted, Ross writes, "evidently determined to sell his life as dearly as possible." In that report, unlike his 1880s account, the chief was not involuntarily pulled from his horse by the fall of a dying girl. No mention of a girl riding behind a chief exists in the 1870s letter. The double-riding girl first appeared in the 1880s account to DeShields. There is also no mention in the report to Governor Houston of Ross's killing a chief.

In the early 1870s Ross claims he killed chief Mohee and does not mention any help from a Mexican servant, which he does in the 1880s account. In fact, the only mention of the Mexican servant in the 1870s letter occurs when Ross returns to camp and calls on the servant to interpret what the captives would tell them. In the same 1870s account, not only does Ross write nothing about help from his servant in killing the chief, but also he does not mention a servant being present at the time the chief was being killed.

Thus, in the 1870s in his "correct history" Ross writes that he killed Mohee, but a decade later he tells James DeShields the chief he killed was Peta Nocona.[22] By then, the 1880s, Peta Nocona and Naudah's (Parker's) son Quanah had become famous. Also by that time Peta Nocona, who was once described as a "great, greasy lazy buck," had been transformed. According to the famous scout and interpreter Horace Jones, who knew him, Peta Nocona "was not a chief as some of the [whites] supposed" nor was he "one of the 'big men' among the Indians." Texas Panhandle pioneer Charles Goodnight, who was a friend of Quanah, said Peta Nocona was never a chief. Nor does Nocona's name appear on contemporary lists of Comanche chiefs and headmen. But now, according to Ross, he was a chief and "noted warrior of great repute."[23]

Mohee had vanished. His name no longer appeared in Ross's accounts. His name, it seems, was lost in Ross's political dust that still partially obscures facts surrounding the Pease River battle and Parker's capture. Clearly, political spin is not a modern invention.

In what in essence is another Ross account, Tom Padgitt, Ross's brother-in-law, wrote a letter to the *Dallas Morning News*. Padgitt, who in 1878 had married Ross's sister Kate, wanted to refute a statement Quanah had recently made at the 1909 annual State Fair of Texas. Quanah had said his father was not killed in the Mule Creek fight. Padgitt was not at the Battle of Pease River, but he claimed he received his information from Ross "both at home and around the camp fire."[24] We do not know when Ross provided such information to Padgitt, but probably Padgitt received it over a period of many years. What seems obvious, however, is that in the telling either Ross or Padgitt himself confused the Pease River battle with the 1858 fight at Wichita Village. In his letter to the *Dallas Morning News*, for example, Padgitt claimed Ross "organized a company of his selection, half of which were white and the other half friendly Indians." According to his letter, the company had as its guide "the old friendly Indian Placadore."[25]

Of course, there were no "friendly Indians" in Ross's company at Mule Creek. What is interesting to note is that in his 1920 account, Peter Robertson specifically denied that there were friendly Indians involved in the fight: "there were no friendly Indians in the outfit," he said.[26] Does his statement indicate he was familiar with Padgett's erroneous claim? As suggested throughout this book, it is obvious that many of the participants or alleged participants were familiar with the accounts of the fight as described by others. Also, as noted by Ross and others, in the 1858 fight at the Wichita village the Ross command included Indians as both members in his company and as guides.

Padgitt's account of the fight along Mule Creek differs from Ross's authorized account. Padgitt claims the chief jumped off his horse. Ross, on the other hand, wrote that a girl who was riding behind the chief and who had been killed instantly by a pistol shot from Ross pulled the chief off the horse. According to Padgitt's 1909 letter, the girl remained on the horse and Ross rode past her and, seeing that he had shot her, allowed her to go on, a benevolent action that even Ross does not claim.

Also, Tom Padgitt incorrectly claims, "The first roof that sheltered Cynthia Ann Parker in twenty-four years, after her return to civilization was the old Ross home." Parker never stayed in the Ross home. On the return trip from the battle, Sergeant Spangler took Parker and her daughter to Camp Cooper, and Ross returned to Waco to meet with Governor Houston. After her uncle Colonel Isaac Parker identified her at Camp Cooper, she went to live with members of the Parker family.

Padgitt's letter was designed to defend Sul Ross and the authorized account, which stated Ross had killed Peta Nocona. Padgitt obviously was careless and uninformed. He did not substantiate some of the information he reported and took considerable license to support his brother-in-law. Indeed, carelessness and literary license are characteristic of many of those who report on the Battle of Pease River.

Other differences in the reports of Sul Ross exist. In the 1861 report to Houston, Ross has Tom Kelliher chasing the person later discovered to be Cynthia Ann Parker, and Ross was not involved in the chase. In the same report it was Lieutenant Kelliher who was about to shoot Parker when she showed the baby and cried "Americano." By the mid-1880s not only had Ross become part of the chase, but also he had become the rider who was in the act of shooting when Parker held up the child.

In his 1870s letter published in the *Galveston News* and the *Dallas Weekly Herald* in 1875, Ross states Kelliher chased Parker, and he and Lieutenant Somerville chased another Indian, who Ross reported was a chief. He writes, "two Indians, well mounted, attempted to escape," and Kelliher chased one, who turned out to be Parker, and Ross and Somerville chased the other, who turned out to be Mohee.

And again, in his 1861 report to Governor Houston, Ross claims "about forty head of animals were taken." It is the same number Ross gave to the *Herald*'s correspondent in December 1860, for the newspaperman reported "about 40 head of horses were taken." By the early 1870s Ross had increased the number of horses to 350. Several writers and one alleged former Texas Ranger adopted the larger figure.[27]

Then there is the problem of the double-riding girl. As noted in chapter 2, Jonathan Hamilton Baker kept a diary in which he wrote that when he first arrived on the battleground, "We found only four dead Indians, all [women]."[28] Later in his diary, after two days of searching the area, Baker writes, "We cannot find but seven Indians killed, four [women] and three [men]."[29]

If the diary is correct, and if Sul Ross had killed a girl riding behind a chief, as he claims in the authorized account, Baker's group never found the body of the double-riding girl. Her body should have been very close to the chief's body, and according to all accounts everyone knew the location of his body. In Baker's diary the death count for Indian women never rose after the initial four were found at the time Baker first arrived on the battleground. If the girl was one of the initial four, how did Cureton's militiamen miss the body of the chief, which must have been close to the girl's body?

The girl on the back of the horse was not mentioned in Ross's 1861 report to Governor Houston. The girl did not appear in the 1870s letter. In the letter, Ross stated that "two Indians . . . attempted to escape. . . . [Kelliher] . . . started in pursuit of one, and . . . Somerville and myself after the other." Maybe there was no double-riding girl at all, and Ross realized that he had killed a girl, knowingly or not. If so, perhaps he determined it would be better to have the girl unintentionally shot on the back of the chief's horse, especially if that chief was "a noted warrior of great repute." In any event, her body should have been found close to that of the chief and Baker's count of dead women raised to five if in fact she was with the chief. According to his brother-in-law, Ross said he allowed the girl to ride on after she was shot.[30]

The girl's fate is connected with Lieutenant M. W. Somerville's problems with the chief as mentioned in Ross's 1861 report to Houston. "Dismounting," as the report states, and "evidently determined to sell his life as dearly as possible" are poor descriptions of someone who supposedly was involuntarily pulled off his horse by the fall of a dying girl. In the authorized account neither Somerville nor any other Texas Ranger was present when the chief was pulled from his horse. Is it possible that by the mid-1880s Ross had assumed a few of Somerville's experiences as his own?

In evaluating the various Ross reports, one should consider other participant accounts of Ross's alleged fight with the chief. One of them is the narrative of Peter Robertson, who gave a brief description of the fight between Ross and the chief. "Peta Nocona tried to rally his men and make a stand," said Robertson. "Seeing his efforts, Ross charged him, and it was then the hand-to-hand fight with the chief came off. I didn't see much of this fight between Ross and Old Peta, as just at that time I was mighty busy. When Ross dashed on him he was using his six-shooter, while the Indian tried to unhorse him with his lance." Robertson also reported, "Ross killed the chief's horse, and when the animal fell the Indian threw his lance at Ross . . . which struck [Ross's] horse's tail and this made the steed so ungovernable that Ross had to dismount. . . . The last shot in his pistol was fired, breaking the chief's arm. He then drew his sword and advanced on the infuriated savage, who, with his shield, warded off the cuts and thrusts." Robertson then concluded, "At this stage of the game, some of the boys fired on the Indian and killed him, and as he went down he struck his head against a cottonwood tree that stood near on the bank of the creek. The man who shot the Indian was some fifty or seventy-five yards away when he fired, and I afterwards heard Ross say to him, 'You made a splendid shot.'"[31]

Another description came from Ranger Ben Dragoo: "Ross had a fight at close quarters with a chief, and it happened right in the village," Dragoo said. "During the scrap with the chief, Ross was wounded and told [his] Mexican [servant] to shoot [the chief]. The Mexican . . . shot the Indian through the hips. This brought the chief to a sitting posture and while making the most horrid faces and defying his conquerors by grimace, and every other taunting gesture known to savages, one of our men . . . ran up and knocked him on the head with his gun." He concluded, "With his knife, and while the old savage was still kicking, he made a quick incision around his head from ear to ear, and when he jerked off his scalp it popped like a rifle." Just as Robertson had read others' accounts of the battle, so had Dragoo. He stated, for example, "And as to that death song tale if that chief sang a death song that day, it was after we left him—dead."[32]

Both Robertson and Dragoo say the battle with the chief happened in the village and not some two miles away as Ross claims. Both argue the chief was actually killed by a member of the Texas Rangers: Robertson claims with a "splendid shot" from fifty to seventy-five yards away, and Dragoo with a hit on the head. In addition, Robertson claims Ross's horse was injured by a lance, but Ross states the injury to his horse came from an arrow.

Several writers have described Ross's fight with the chief as being a "hand-to-hand" encounter. Probably the first such description appears in the January 1861 edition of the *Galveston Civilian*.[33] If "hand-to-hand" means at close quarters, then the description of the fight as related by Robertson appears to fit that meaning more closely than do Ross's later accounts. Attacking a person with a sword appears to be more hand-to-hand than does shooting the person when he is on the ground and you are sitting on a horse. Of course, it is possible the "hand-to-hand" references are nothing more than heroic rhetoric.

Where was the so-called "hand-to-hand" fight, in the village or two miles away after a hard chase? And were the Texas Rangers' horses up to a two-mile chase? In 1861 Ross reported to Governor Houston, "Not more than twenty [Rangers] were able to get in the fight, owing to the starved and jaded condition of their horses, having had no grass after leaving the vicinity of Belknap, except 'dry sedge,' which the buffalo had refused."[34] Were the horses of the Rangers who were able to get in the fight in much better shape?

According to former Texas Ranger Benjamin Franklin Gholson, Ross was not sure. Gholson, who may have fabricated his recollections, claims that after the Indians were discovered, Ross stated, "Mr. Stuart, you go back as hurriedly as you can till you meet Captain Cureton, tell him the Indians are breaking camp and going off and we've got to attack, for if they get away we cannot overtake them on account of the condition of our horses."[35]

The narratives of both Robertson and Dragoo contradict Ross's accounts in many important details, and they do not appear to be the kind of details that can be readily passed off as being caused by a faulty memory. They appear to be more in keeping with the deliberate falsification of facts. In other words, someone is lying. We know Dragoo's claim to being a childhood playmate of Cynthia Ann Parker and his claim concerning Quanah cannot be believed, but what about his description of the battle?

Ross's authorized account in James T. DeShields's *Cynthia Ann Parker* was given sometime in the mid- to early 1880s. Having been born in September 1838, Ross was in his mid-forties at the time, and twenty to twenty-five years had passed since the Pease River battle. Consequently, his memory of the events should have been clearer than the memories of Peter Robertson or Ben Dragoo. As early as 1878, however, Ross was telling his friend Victor Rose that his memory was defective and worthless as to some Civil War events.[36]

Robertson and Dragoo at the time they reported on the Mule Creek incident were older than Ross. Robertson's story was given about 1920 and, assuming he was at least twenty years of age at the time of the battle, Robertson would have been at least eighty years old at the time he provided his narrative. Dragoo's account was printed in the December 1923 edition of *Frontier Times*, but there is no mention of the date he gave it. In 1923 Dragoo would have been about eighty-eight years of age, and he was still giving interviews as late as December 1927.

The most obvious changes in Sul Ross's story occurred between the early 1870s and the mid-1880s. During that important time in Ross's political life, Mohee became Peta Nocona. But there were other changes, although minor.

In the 1890s Ross gave an informal account to Susan Parker St. John, daughter of Nathaniel Parker and first cousin to Cynthia Ann Parker. St. John in 1894 visited with Ross while he served as president of Texas A&M. Ross told her about the Battle of Pease River, indicated the story had been told many times, and said the James DeShields account depicted the capture of Parker about as it occurred. Not satisfied with the answer, St. John asked Ross to tell her what he remembered. The former Texas Ranger captain then told her, "Well DeShields' account is almost correct. Nocona did not sing as he says, and it was John Spangler who caught Cynthia Ann's pony. He was going to shoot when she held up her baby, and tearing open her clothes bared her bosom saying Americano, Americano."[37]

Of course, the former Ranger's last two statements to Susan St. John contradict all of his previous accounts of either the death song story or the name of the person who captured Parker. What Ross told St. John confirms Ben Dragoo's statement that the alleged chief did not sing a death song. Before his conversation with St. John, one should recall,

Sul Ross, ca. 1890. Courtesy of Texas Collection, Baylor University, Waco, Texas.

Ross gave sole "credit" for the capture to Tom Kelliher. And one should also recall Charles Loeffler's 1908 argument that he, Loeffler, effected the capture of Parker. Loeffler's claim prompted the assistant adjutant general to publish Ross's report to Governor Sam Houston, the point of which was to give credit to Kelliher.

Ross appears to tell St. John it was DeShields who made mistakes. But of the people whom DeShields credits for his information, only Ross was present at the battle. DeShields, of course, was capable of hyperbole and fiction, and his statements might have been the sole product of his imagination. The problem, however, is one fears DeShields intended both his hyperbole and fiction to be taken as fact; he told his readers that his book was a "narrative of plain unvarnished facts." Perhaps he lied. Ross, who possibly expected and desired the embellishment, may have thought DeShields's authorized account aided his political ambitions to such an extent that it would be counterproductive to make corrections until a later date.

What about Ross's report to Sam Houston? It was made only two weeks after the battle, and in it Ross says Kelliher, a Texas Ranger, caught Parker, a claim that is repeated in his account contained in the Ross Family Papers. The Ross Family Papers also contain information about the death song, which is further evidence the Ross Family Papers were written after DeShields's book appeared and to some extent were taken from the book. Not until 1894 did Ross admit that federal troopers and not Kelliher took Parker. Why he would report to Governor Houston otherwise is a question that can be answered only by speculation.

Another matter should be discussed. Ross not only changed the number of Texas Rangers involved in the fight, but he also changed the number of the federal troops who participated. The cavalry numbers went from three in his report to Houston to twenty in his 1870s letter in the 1875 *Galveston News* and *Dallas Weekly Herald*. As noted in chapter 2, Sergeant John Spangler of the cavalry was uncertain about the number of Rangers involved in the fight. Remember he first reported "during the fight we had the assistance of Captain Ross, Lieutenants [Kelliher] and Sublett with about ten of [Ross's] men."[38] Also recall, in his second report he claimed that at the time of the charge he did not see more than five or six Rangers. It is possible that Spangler's first report of about thirteen and Ross's report of not more than twenty are approximately the same and reflect close to the true number of Rangers involved in the fight.[39]

In summary, the Battle of Pease River and the 1860 capture of Cynthia Ann Parker to a significant extent impacted Ross's subsequent life. Clearly, Sul Ross had more to gain in having his account told and accepted than did Robertson, Dragoo, or any other person involved in the fight. Ross used his role in the battle to advance his political ambitions, asking his friend Victor M. Rose to embellish the story in a political sketch produced during his 1880 run for state senator. In 1886, James T. DeShields with dramatic effect did the same thing when Ross sought the governor's office. Moreover, as his political interests increased, Ross took full advantage of the growing fame of Quanah, Cynthia Ann Parker's son, to promote his career. Thus, in 1886 DeShields had Ross kill Peta Nocona, Quanah's father and "a noted warrior of great repute," rather than Mohee, as Ross had previously claimed.

Not all of Ross's contemporaries bought into such political spin. According to J. Frank Dobie, Ross's "vote-seeking . . . lessened him in Charles Goodnight's eyes." Dobie writes of a 1919 trip Goodnight took with H. B. Willis. As they approached Waco, Willis asked Goodnight if he wished to go by Ross's place. Goodnight replied, "Why in hell would I want to see anything connected with that old lying four-flusher named Sul Ross."[40]

Just as clearly, the myth of the battle as portrayed by DeShields in 1886 quickly became part of the state's collective memory. The myth was too strong in 1908 to shake even editors of Texas newspapers from their confidence in the truth of the wrong date for the fight. And in later years no one seemed to question the myth that Ross killed Peta Nocona. Alone, these two examples affirm a tradition and folklore that turned a massacre into a great and defining battle. Together with additional misunderstandings and errors in reporting, they created a Texas collective memory of the Battle of Pease River and the 1860 capture of Cynthia Ann Parker worthy of a mythic nineteenth-century Texas.

# 4

## THE REMINISCENCES
## Benjamin F. Gholson

T here is a great deal of history in myth and folklore, which is good. But sometimes there is too much folklore and myth in history. Concerning the Battle of Pease River, for example, the error-filled interviews or reminiscences of Benjamin Franklin "Frank" Gholson have contributed far more to myth and folklore than to history. Unfortunately, Gholson's documents have frequently been accepted as authentic eyewitness descriptions of the event, even the history of it. The faulty Gholson statements in other words too often represent the traditional knowledge—Texans' historic memory—of the fight along Mule Creek and the 1860 capture of Cynthia Ann Parker.

In their use as historical documents, Gholson's reminiscences run second only to Sul Ross's authorized account. In many books and articles related to the one-sided battle, the authors have cited Gholson as one of their authorities, and sometimes their principal authority.[1] Consequently, Gholson's claim to having been one of the Texas Rangers who participated in the fight at Mule Creek, the statements he gave to support that claim, and his descriptions of the events themselves warrant close examination, for the lively storyteller did not participate in the Battle of Pease River.

Benjamin Gholson was born November 17, 1842. He lived in several Texas counties before settling near Evant in Lampasas County, where he became a rancher and farmer. As a young man he served from April 1 to August 16, 1859, in John Williams's Texas Ranger company and later enlisted in what became known as Sul Ross's first company. Captain J. M. Smith had originally organized the company, but after Smith received a promotion, Ross through election became the company captain, his first such command.

Gholson gave at least two statements concerning the Battle of Pease River. Although the statements have been referred to as "interviews," the interviewers do not appear to have questioned him in either incident. Instead, they allowed Gholson to provide a running narrative or statement of his experiences. He gave the first statement to J. A. Rickard in August 1928, some sixty-seven years after the battle, when Gholson was eighty-five years old. He gave the second to Felix Williams and Harvey Chelsey in August 1931, three years later. Scholars and others who write on the famous battle cite the second interview most often.[2]

Nowhere does Gholson claim to have seen all that he reports. Yet in the spirit of Lord St. John's advice to Tom Canty in *The Prince and the Pauper*, Gholson remembers all he can and seems to remember all else. As for those events and conversations he did not personally see or hear, he claims to have received his information from others. His accounts of many events and conversations are, therefore, not based on his personal observations but rather on his memory of what others told him sixty-eight or seventy-one years previously. Equally troubling is the possibility his reminiscences may be based on what he heard or read many years after the battle.

In his 1928 statement Gholson says: "I had been forced to secure an

Ben Gholson, ca. 1920. Reprinted by permission of
Texas Ranger Hall of Fame and Museum, Waco.

honorable discharge from Captain Sul Ross' first company and return home early in 1859 on account of the death of my father." The reference to 1859 is no doubt a mistake and it should be 1860, for it was in 1860 that his father died and the year Ross became captain of the company originally organized under J. M. Smith.[3] Such errors are not serious, granted, but they represent examples of Gholson's difficulties in remembering. Could such problems also extend to Gholson's memory of events about which he learned through conversation and hearsay?

Although each of the Gholson interviews includes some tales that are unique, the two statements have much in common. Both contain the following information: The Comanches had started to leave their village when the Texas Rangers and federal troops attacked on December 18—the wrong date, of course. Sergeant John W. Spangler and his twenty federal troopers rode to cut off the Indians' escape. The Comanche chief turned back with some of his warriors and formed an oblong circle in which the warriors dismounted and used their horses for breastworks. Upon orders from Captain Sul Ross, Gholson and eleven other Rangers went in pursuit of some Comanches who were attempting to escape.

As a result of the pursuit, Gholson left the battle scene. Thus, he did not personally see or hear any of the events or conversations he described pertaining to the battle and the capture of Cynthia Ann Parker. He got such information, he claimed, from other Texas Rangers. Nonetheless, Gholson in both interviews continued the story as if he had been there. He said that after many of the warriors in the oblong circle had been either killed or wounded, the chief ordered the remaining Comanches to mount the nearest horse and flee. After the chief mounted his horse, a girl jumped on the same animal and rode behind him. When leaving the circle, the chief shot an arrow at Lieutenant M. W. Somerville, a Texas Ranger who was directly in the chief's line of departure. Sommerville ducked and the arrow missed him. Thereupon,

Sul Ross chased the chief and the girl. Ross shot the girl, who, when falling from the horse, pulled the chief to the ground. The chief let loose numerous arrows at Ross, and Ross fired several pistol shots at the chief, hitting the Comanche leader two or three times. In Gholson's 1928 statement one of Ross's bullets broke the chief's leg, but in the 1931 statement Ross's shot broke the chief's arm, a claim consistent with one of the Ross accounts of the incident.

In either event, both Gholson interviews say the chief was disabled and leaned against a tree. At that moment Ross's Mexican servant, who, according to Gholson, at one time had been a captive and personal slave of the chief and could speak the Comanche language, arrived on the scene. Gholson said the Mexican servant indicated the chief was Peta Nocona, and he was talking to his god. Ross told his servant to tell the chief that if he surrendered he would not be shot again. The chief said he would surrender when he was dead and thrust his spear at Ross. The Ranger captain easily avoided the deadly weapon.

Ross, Gholson's narratives continue, said the chief was the bravest man he had ever seen and he could not shoot him. Thereupon, the servant shot the chief. After looking at the dead Comanche leader, Ross rode off to check on Lieutenant Tom Kelliher, who was having some difficulty with another Comanche, the person who turned out to be Cynthia Ann Parker. The Mexican servant ran up and identified her as the chief's wife. Before capturing her, Kelliher had been in the act of shooting her when she held up a baby and said "Americano." Later, the captured woman wanted to go to where the chief was killed. When allowed to go there, she paraded around the chief's body and paid respects to the dead girl. Texas Rangers had to force her away.

In short, such is a synopsis of those portions of the Gholson reminiscences that are essentially the same. The 1928 statement is much longer and more detailed than the 1931 interview, but other than the discrepancy about which of the chief's bones was broken, there are few differences between them. Perhaps between 1928 and 1931 Gholson had read the Ross account that mentions breaking the Comanche leader's arm, and that refreshed Gholson's memory about what he may have read or heard.

Under scrutiny the reminiscences wither. Perhaps the most troublesome issues are references to the number of Comanches at Mule Creek. In 1931 Gholson claimed he saw between 500 and 600 Indians, 150 to 200 of whom were warriors. He does not provide a number for Indians killed, but he indicates that the Texas Rangers and federal troopers did not kill or capture all of them. He says, however, that seventeen Indians died in the oblong circle. As the chief and the girl also died, the 1931 number of people dead reaches at least nineteen.

In the long 1928 recitation, Gholson does not provide a figure for the number of Indians in the village, but he offers a total number for Comanches pursued and killed. The figures are contained in his description of the chase he and the other eleven Texas Rangers with the best horses made. He says they pursued the escaping Comanches about twelve miles, after which they stopped and, apparently, counted the number of Indians they had been chasing. He indicates they saw seventy Indians sitting on their horses. The seventy were carrying another thirty-two people who were either dead or wounded. On their return trip to the battleground the Rangers discovered seven other Comanches "either dead or wounded."

To summarize, Gholson says that twelve Rangers on jaded horses chased at least 109 Comanches, including warriors, about twelve miles and made the return trip, for a total of twenty-four miles, without difficulty. The Rangers killed or wounded thirty-nine Indians, and those Comanches who had not been either killed or wounded were able, during the chase, to recover thirty-two of the dead or injured. If it is true, the chase and return effort deserves high praise indeed, even if the Rangers were on strong, fresh horses. Recall, however, that on at least two occasions Ross wrote that the Rangers' horses at times had subsisted entirely on the bark and small limbs of cottonwood trees and were in poor condition. Also, in his 1928 statement Gholson claimed Ross said, "We've got to attack, for if [the Comanches] get away we cannot overtake them on account of the condition of our horses."[4]

In the same statement Gholson indicated that, when they started for home, the Texas Rangers had the scalps of twenty-six Comanches but had left one dead warrior's hair unmolested. He was not scalped, Gholson says, because the captured woman had shown more grief over his body than she did the others, and the Rangers thought the dead person might be her son.

The large Gholson numbers vary from those of other participants. On the day of the fight, for example, Sul Ross told J. J. "Jack" Cureton's militiamen that the Rangers and troopers had overtaken a party of fifteen Indians and had killed twelve of them and taken three prisoners.[5] Four days after the battle, Ross told a correspondent for the *Dallas Herald* that his command had killed thirteen Indians and taken three prisoners, and, whether Ross told him or not, the correspondent reported the entire party of Indians had been either killed or captured.[6] And then on January 4, 1861, Ross reported to Governor Sam Houston that the Comanche village consisted of eight or nine grass tents with fifteen Indians present.[7]

Sergeant Spangler of the Second Cavalry and Jonathan Baker also gave numbers that conflicted with Gholson's account. On December 24, 1860, Spangler wrote that about twenty-five Indians were in the village.[8] Jonathan Baker noted in his diary that, after two days of investigating the extended battleground, he and others of Cureton's command could find the bodies of only seven people.[9]

In his 1928 statement Gholson mentions a horse herd, but not any specific number of Indian horses captured. He corrected the oversight in 1931, for then he claims they captured 370 Indian horses and mules.

As mentioned, Sul Ross twice claimed his party captured about forty horses, John Spangler reported capturing forty-five animals, and Jonathan Baker claimed about thirty horses and mules captured.[10]

Against any of these reports Gholson's numbers for Comanches present and killed and for horses and mules captured seem greatly inflated. For the erroneous Indian numbers no explanation seems apparent. For the horse numbers there may at least be an explanation of the source. If Gholson changed his 1931 testimony after reading Ross's story about shattering the chief's arm, perhaps he had also read or heard about Ross's 1875 claim in the Galveston and Dallas newspapers about killing or scattering 350 horses. Of course, by making such a report Ross inflated and contradicted two of his own accounts, both made within sixteen days of the battle.

Clearly, Gholson's numbers are based on what he had read rather than on his personal observations, as is his description of the chief talking to his god or reciting a death song. The death song story first appeared in 1886 in DeShields's biography of Parker, and it remained the only such story until Gholson told it almost verbatim from the book in his reminiscences. The death song did not happen; DeShields fabricated it to embellish his book. In writing of the event he supposedly quoted Sul Ross, but in 1894 Ross told Susan Parker St. John that DeShields's book was in error in two respects, one of which was the death song story. Texas Ranger Ben Dragoo also denied the death song, saying, "As to that death song tale, if that chief sang that day it was after we left him—dead."[11] The reasonable deduction is that Gholson got the story from DeShields's book—the same place he got the wrong date of the battle.

Gholson's story has other questionable issues, including the Texas Ranger pursuit of 109 escaping Indians. According to Gholson, Sul Ross, after the brief fight near the village, did not wait for the twelve Texas Rangers to return from their pursuit but instead with his re-

Pease River looking west in 2008 from a prominent peak.
Photograph courtesy of Monte L. Monroe.

Mule Creek from near its mouth in 2008. Photograph courtesy of Bryan Edwards.

Confluence of Mule Creek and Pease River, ca. 2008.
Photograph courtesy of Bryan Edwards.

maining eight Rangers and the federal troopers left the battlefield and started back down the Pease River to meet Cureton's command. And after meeting with Ross, the militiamen rode to the battle site, where, according to Gholson, they arrived before the twelve Rangers had returned.

If he is correct, Gholson's account reflects unfavorably on Ross's concern for the welfare of his Rangers. According to Gholson, Ross left the battlefield not knowing the location or fate of twelve of his twenty men, who the last time he saw them were in pursuit of 109 Comanches. Of course, if there were only fifteen Indians in the Comanche camp, as Ross stated, the Ranger captain would not have hesitated to leave the field without the twelve Rangers. Or, if there was no chase, there were no Rangers on whom to wait.

The oblong circle tale is also problematic. Benjamin Gholson's accounts are the only ones to describe the circle. In both 1928 and 1931 Gholson claimed he saw Indians form the defensive circle, but because he participated in the twelve-mile chase he did not witness what happened at the circle. He got the story from Texas Rangers or more likely fabricated it. Recall that Ross reported to Governor Houston, "Many of [the Comanches] were killed before they could make any preparation for defense. Several, however, were well mounted and succeeded in getting about two miles from the village before they were killed." Ross does not mention Indian warriors forming an oblong circle. Neither does Sergeant Spangler of the Second Cavalry.[12] In his account of the battle, Ben Dragoo states: "Some [Comanches] were trying to rally their braves, others were mounted, some on foot, women and children were screaming." He does not mention a circle or that the Comanches were successful in any way in attempting to rally their men.[13]

Peter Robertson says, "When we made the charge most of the Indians had mounted. . . . We took them by surprise and they didn't have much show for a fight. . . . Peta Nocona tried to rally his men and make a stand. Seeing his efforts, Ross charged him, and it is then the hand-to-hand fight with the chief came off."[14] Robertson's account is a mixed blessing to those who rely on Benjamin Gholson for their description of the battle. The Robertson statement, "Peta Nocona tried to rally his men and make a stand," might support Gholson's argument that the chief ordered his men to take a defensive position, perhaps to form an oblong circle. Robertson, however, has Ross, upon seeing the chief's effort to rally his men, charge the chief and engage him in hand-to-hand combat before killing him. In Robertson's version the chief neither escaped nor nearly shot Lieutenant M. W. Somerville.

Gholson's statements about the oblong circle and twelve-mile chase are troublesome in other ways. Not more than twenty Texas Rangers were present during the fight. Gholson says, however, that he and eleven others were chasing 109 Comanches. If Gholson is correct, consequently, no more than eight Rangers plus Ross were available to confront more than seventeen Indians in the circle; the federal troops were off chasing other Indians. Of course, if he thought twelve Rangers were sufficient to take on 109 Comanches, Ross may have thought he and eight other Rangers could handle seventeen Indian warriors.

The Gholson reminiscences leave a number of questions. Does it seem plausible that Sul Ross would attack a party of between 500 and 600 Comanches, 150 to 200 of them warriors, with a combined command of forty Texas Rangers and federal troopers whose horses were in poor condition? Does it seem probable that Ross, confronting between 500 and 600 Comanches, would split his forty-man force not once but twice, leaving him with no more than eight Rangers to face at least seventeen Indians in a defensive oblong circle? Does it seem probable that Ross would leave the battlefield and abandon twelve of his twenty Rangers, who were out of sight and chasing 109 Indians? In addition, does it seem probable that, after two days of searching, men of Cureton's command would fail to discover the bodies of the seventeen Comanches killed in the oblong circle? If the oblong circle story has any merit, does it not seem logical that both Ross's and Spangler's figure given for the number of Comanches killed would be much greater?

As stated, much of Gholson's information covers material that he did not personally observe or hear, but instead received from other Rangers. He does not identify any specific Ranger who furnished the information, but in the 1928 interview he mentions the names of some surviving Rangers who fought at Pease River. He lists R. B. Fulcher, E. D. Whatley, H. B. Rogers, and Ben Dragoo, whose names are on the muster roll/payroll for the Ranger company that was part of the Pease River expedition. Few people have questioned information in the perplexing Gholson statements that came from the Rangers. On the contrary, although the reminiscences raise sobering questions about Gholson's memory or veracity, many people accept Gholson's comments as unquestioned truth.

Harvey Chelsey, one of the two people who "interviewed" Gholson in 1931, claims Gholson "had a remarkable memory and a high reputation for accuracy." But he also stated, "Anyway, it makes a good story." Probably few people would disagree with Chelsey's latter observation, but many may have reasons to doubt Gholson's "remarkable memory." There may be no reason to doubt Gholson's "reputation for accuracy," but there are valid reasons to doubt his accuracy in fact, as well as his commitment to the truth.[15]

Gholson's memory and accuracy represent troublesome issues, but they are not the only problems with his statements. Some serious issues pertain to his Texas Ranger service. Gholson was a Ranger, and his name appears on the muster roll for Captain John Williams's company of Rangers. He probably served in Ross's first company, but because there is no muster roll for the company his service with it cannot be verified. To qualify for a pension at the time, one needed to complete at least thirty days of active service. Gholson's service with the Williams company was sufficient for him to receive a federal pension for defending the frontier.[16]

On April 16, 1917, Benjamin Gholson applied for a pension. In his application he claimed service in Captain John Williams's company from October 1, 1858, to March 1859.[17] The muster roll for Williams's company indicates Gholson served from April 1, 1859, to August 16, 1859. In spite of the discrepancies in the dates of service, Gholson's request was approved, and he received a pension.[18]

More problematical was Gholson's claim of service in Ross's second company of Texas Rangers, the company involved in the Battle of Pease River. Gholson's name does not appear on the muster roll for that company, which was organized October 3, 1860, and discharged

February 5, 1861. In his sworn application for his pension, Gholson
said he served in the company from September 20, 1860, a date before
it was organized, until the last of March 1861, a date after the company was discharged. The company's muster roll, however, shows that
no member served before September 22, 1860, or after February 5,
1861. Moreover, the adjutant general for Texas in a letter to the commissioner of pensions in Washington, D.C., wrote, "The name of B. F.
[Gholson] does not appear on the roll of Capt. L. S. Ross' Co. Rangers,
Oct. 3, 1860–Feb. 5, 1861."[19]

When he swore he was in Ross's second company, Gholson noted
his service was under the command of S. L. Ross, reversing Ross's
initials. Was it a simple error of transposition? On the previously written line and directly above the reversed initials, when referring to his
service under the earlier Ross company, Gholson wrote the correct initials, L. S., thus indicating he was familiar with the correct order of the
initials.[20]

On July 9, 1917, the pension office sent Gholson another pension-
related form. The second form stated that one of its purposes was
to aid the Bureau of Pensions in preventing anyone from committing
fraud in Gholson's name or on account of his service. On July 27, 1917,
when he completed the second form, Gholson omitted all references to
any service in Ross's second company, although the form provided him
three opportunities to list such service. He mentioned only the John
Williams and earlier Sul Ross companies.[21]

Indeed, Gholson's answers to the questions about his service seem
revealing. In answer to the question, "When did you enlist?" Gholson
answers, "Williams 2nd Co. Oct. 1st, 1858. Ross 1st Co. May 1860.
Smith Co. March, 1860." In answer to this question on his application,
Gholson does not mention Ross's second company, the command that
was involved in the Pease River fight. There also is no mention of an
enlistment on September 20, 1860.

In answer to the question, "When were you discharged?" Gholson answers, "March, 1859, August 1860, May 1860." There is no mention of a discharge date of March 1861, the date mentioned by Gholson for his service under S. L. Ross.

In answer to the question, "The name of organizations in which you served?" Gholson answers, "Williams 2nd Co., Ross' 1st Co., M. T. Johnson Reg., Smith's Co." In March 1860 Governor Houston had authorized Colonel Middleton T. Johnson to form a Ranger command. Five companies initially answered his call. Captain J. M. Smith raised the Waco company, and Sul Ross joined it. In May 1860 Smith became lieutenant colonel of the entire command, and Ross, as indicated, took Smith's position in the Waco company, which was thereafter known as Ross's first company. In reality, Johnson's company, Smith's company, and Ross's first company were all the same, and they disbanded in August 1860.

Did the mention of the word *fraud* in the pension form cause Gholson to rethink his application? When he listed serving in Ross's second company, he reversed Ross's initials and claimed service for a period that started before the company organized and extended past the date the company disbanded. Plus, he made such claims for a company in which his name does not appear on the muster roll.

As he needed only thirty days of service to qualify for a pension, perhaps Gholson decided to drop his claim for service under Ross's second company. If through government mismanagement his name was mistakenly omitted from the muster roll but he qualified for a pension without it, perhaps he determined not to push the matter. No one may know with certainty whether Gholson was in fact a member of Sul Ross's second company, but if one relies on the official record, the answer is no, he was not.

In any case, scholars should be hesitant to rely on the Gholson accounts. Gholson seems to have misremembered, erred, or manufactured events he claims to have seen along Mule Creek. About events he admits he did not see or hear, his commentary is particularly suspect. When one compares Gholson's accounts with those of Sul Ross, John Spangler, Jonathan Baker, Ben Dragoo, and James Robertson, Gholson's memory and accuracy seem flaccid; indeed, they are exceptionally poor.

It is obvious that as early as 1917 Gholson was having trouble remembering the dates of his Texas Ranger service. He missed the date of joining Williams's company by six months and the date of his discharge by five months. Even if he did serve in Ross's second company, he remembered joining before the company was even organized and being discharged a month after it disbanded. At one time in 1928 Gholson could not remember the correct year he joined Ross's first company or the correct year his father died. His number of Comanches, both present and killed, and his number of captured horses suggest that his memory completely failed him. Or, was he simply trying to make his story as entertaining as possible?

If one wishes to assume Gholson was a member of Ross's second company, and that his name was mistakenly omitted from the muster roll, one might conclude Gholson was at Mule Creek. Perhaps, one could argue, he was with the Texas Rangers but not a part of the attacking force. Rather, he was with the twenty-plus Rangers who did not participate because of the poor condition of their horses. If years later he wanted to claim he was in the battle, Gholson might then explain his absence during the fight by inventing the chase scene.

Perhaps there is another possibility. Although his name does not appear on any list of those men who served with Cureton's civilian force, Gholson could have been part of that command. In his diary Jonathan Baker makes note of some men in Cureton's group whose names do not appear on the known lists of that command. While Baker never mentions him, Gholson could have been one of the men whose name failed to make any list.

The evidence shows such assumptions would be wrong. The evidence, rather, indicates that Gholson was nowhere near Mule Creek in December 1860. His interview reports are a product not of his experiences as a member of the Pease River expedition but of his discussions with actual participants, his reading of various Pease River accounts, and his lively imagination. They represent far more fantasy, myth, and folklore than history. The only safe conclusion is that everyone can agree with Harvey Chelsey: Benjamin Gholson tells a good story.

In the final analysis, the real problem with Gholson and his reminiscences is not Gholson. Instead, the problem is with writers and historians who quote him. If such authors had found Ross's earlier reports, Spangler's official reports, or Baker's original diary, they would have known that Gholson's accounts were bogus. However, by relying too heavily on Gholson's accounts, they have perpetuated in the collective memory of Texans a false history of the fight at Pease River. The bluegrass song "Daddy Played the Banjo" suggests, "Memories of what never was become the good old days." One should also recognize that memories of what never was often become a part of a culture's collective memory.

Much has been written and discussed over the years as to the identity of the Comanche warrior or chief Sul Ross fought on the morning of December 19, 1860. Even Ross gave conflicting accounts concerning the person's identity. Such a discussion is important. It helps to explain Ross's changing story about the fight near Pease River, it goes to the heart of Texas myth and the difficulties associated with altering a culture's collective memory, and it is the subject of chapter 5.

# 5
## PETA NOCONA
## The Evidence Examined

In her book *The Gnostic Gospels*, Elaine Pagels advises her readers that, as she understands it, the task of the historian is not to advocate any side but to explore the evidence. Nineteenth-century historian Hubert Howe Bancroft, as quoted in Will Bagley's *Blood of the Prophets*, extends the task to all writers when he states, "Every truthful writer of history must hold himself absolutely free to be led wherever the facts carry him."[1]

Professional historians profess an agreement with such sentiments even if in practice they fail to adhere to the ideal standard. Pagels and Bancroft are not saying that, after having made a diligent and thorough search for the truth, historians and other writers are forbidden to form an opinion based on what the sources reveal. After all, it is not only the historian's duty to make a careful investigation for information but also to interpret the source materials.

Problems arise when historians conduct only cursory searches for information and then offer explanations based on the insufficient investigations. Similar problems arise when writers have a preconceived position or argument and present only evidence that supports the contention. In a related sense, such writers may offer only contrary evidence they believe they can effectively disprove. It does not require a great advocate to win an argument if the only evidence offered is that which the advocate chooses to present.

Such problems have arisen on matters dealing with the fight at Pease River, at least with one of the older issues: the identity of the Comanche warrior or chief Sul Ross fought near Mule Creek. A seemingly unshakable myth identifies the Comanche leader as Peta Nocona, the husband of Cynthia Ann Parker and the father of Quanah, perhaps the most famous Comanche chief. Quanah, or Quanah Parker when he added his mother's family name after settling on the Indian Territory reservation, repeatedly said his father was not killed along Mule Creek. Comanche oral tradition makes the same claim.[2]

Yet the myth of Peta Nocona's death at Mule Creek persists. If for no reason except political gain, one can understand why Sul Ross wanted the slain person to be, as Ross himself called Peta Nocona, "a noted warrior of great repute."[3] Moreover, by the late 1870s and early 1880s Quanah's high reputation had become established. In the charged Indian-hating atmosphere of the time, having killed the father of the influential Quanah would bring credit to Ross, particularly among a good portion of the voting public. At least Ross believed so, and thus in the mid-1880s, just in time for Ross's campaign for governor, the dead chief, who until then Ross had claimed was named Mohee, became Peta Nocona.

What is more difficult to understand is the almost fanatical zeal with which others have supported Ross's claim that he killed Quanah's father. Ross's personal and political reasons for saying he killed Peta Nocona cannot be transferred to other writers who support the Ross claim. In

1909 Tom Padgitt, anxious to defend his brother-in-law's later version of the battle, wrote his previously mentioned letter to the *Dallas Morning News*. The purpose of the letter was to refute a claim by Quanah Parker that Ross had not killed Peta Nocona at Mule Creek. This is the letter in which Padgitt indicated that Ross mentioned the Ross–Peta Nocona fight to him "both at home and around the camp fire."[4] Padgitt presented his account as a correction of what he considered to be false representations of what he "knew" were the facts as related to him by his brother-in-law.

One might understand Padgitt's desire to protect the reputation of his wife's brother, but others have been just as anxious to "set the record straight," defend the authorized account, and claim that in December 1860 Ross killed Peta Nocona. Of the others, Robert H. Williams is the most forthright. In 1972 *Texana*, then a quarterly journal, published an article by Williams titled "The Case for Peta Nocona."[5] As the title suggests, Williams writes as if he is making a legal presentation supporting his thesis. The influential article has been cited in several publications, and once it was described as a "convincing discussion of the issue."[6]

Robert Williams sees his article as the product of careful research. Much of his information, however, comes from DeShields's *Cynthia Ann Parker* and from Gholson's August 26, 1931, interview with Felix Williams and Harvey Chelsey.[7] He views Gholson's account as being particularly important to his contention that Peta Nocona died at Pease River.

Williams refers to the Gholson account as "the famous Benjamin Franklin Gholson interview."[8] The interview is indeed well known by authors who have written on the Battle of Pease River, but, unlike Williams, not everyone has accepted its version of events. To establish the account's merit, Williams selected and used parts of Harvey Chelsey's comments about Gholson. The selected portions read: "Mr. Gholson had a remarkable memory, and a high reputation for accuracy," and

Gholson "says . . . the Mexican, Anton, was well acquainted with No-cona, had been his captive and personal slave, and recognized him on the spot just before [Peta Nocona] was killed. Uncle Frank [Gholson] seemed to be certain it was Nocona, and I don't know any better authority. The boys related the incident to him right after it happened."

Williams omitted some of Chelsey's comments. In particular, he left out Chelsey's concession that "Mr. J. Marvin Hunter and, I believe, Dr. Robert T. Hill, each told me that the Indian killed, as related by Mr. Gholson, was not Nocona, but was some other prominent Indian warrior." Williams also omitted the editor's closing comment: "Anyhow, it makes a good story." The Hunter and Hill statements are evidence contrary to his contention, of course, and perhaps Williams felt the last sentence reflects some misgivings about Gholson's story on the part of Chelsey.[9]

As noted in chapter 4, the Chelsey interview contains many problems. It is the one in which Gholson said there were between 500 and 600 Comanches at Mule Creek and 150 or 200 of them were warriors, statements which Williams does not acknowledge. In the same interview, Gholson, in all probability, adopted Sul Ross's 1870s statement about the number of Indian ponies, for he says there were 370 horses and mules captured.[10] If Harvey Chelsey knew more thoroughly the history of the Battle of Pease River, the Gholson claims would have caused him serious misgivings, especially about Gholson's memory and accuracy.

Merits of the Gholson interview aside, Robert H. Williams bases his argument that Sul Ross killed Peta Nocona primarily on three allegations. The first and foremost is Quanah Parker's alleged statement to John Wesley, a local landowner and regional historian, that Quanah's father was killed at Pease River. The second is Ross's claim in his authorized account that he killed Peta Nocona. The third is Gholson's confirmation of the Ross statement. The *Texana* article contains supporting information, of course, including arguments refuting claims by Quanah Parker that his father was not killed at Pease River and interpretations Williams made of comments and actions by Cynthia Ann Parker.

The arguments and interpretations warrant a response, beginning with the key Wesley-Quanah conversation. Williams begins the article, "Comanche Chief Quanah Parker is said to have stated on at least one occasion his father, the famous Chief Peta Nocona, was killed at the Battle of Pease River, on Mule Creek. This statement is highly significant because Parker's denials many years later are the principal foundation for the current belief that Nocona was not the chief whom Sul Ross killed there."[11]

The "at least one occasion" to which Williams refers exists in a newspaper column written by John Wesley, whom Williams describes as being Foard County's "earliest permanent settler." According to Williams the Wesley column appeared in the December 13, 1918, edition of the *Foard County News*. Citing the article, Williams quotes Wesley as follows: "I became acquainted with Quanah Parker in 1882 or 1883 and met him quite often in Vernon where he and members of his tribe came to trade. He was very friendly and wanted to know all about his kinfolks in Parker County. He asked me to visit him at Ft. Sill and I in return asked him to visit me, but he said he never went to Mule Creek because his father was killed there and his mother and brother were captured and carried off. He said he never wanted to see the place."[12]

But there is some confusion. Williams writes in *Texana*: "Wesley's own article, quoted earlier herein, indicated that his invitation and Parker's rejection took place in the early 1890s." Later in his article Williams states it was in the early 1880s, but he does not cite Wesley's article or any other source for the new, earlier date.[13] Did he make a mistake on the date, or was one of the dates a typographical error? If so, which date?

Was Williams basing his allegation, that Quanah's comment about

Quanah Parker on horseback, ca. 1897. The woman to his right is one of his wives.
The others are unidentified. Photograph courtesy of Donald Tabb.

his father's death was made in the early 1880s, on nothing more than Wesley's statement that he "became acquainted with Quanah Parker in 1882 or 1883"? If so, did Williams simply assume, for the sake of his position, that the invitation and rejection took place when Wesley first became acquainted with Quanah Parker and not sometime later in their relationship? As Williams writes, the Wesley article itself states the comment was made in the early 1890s. Why would he then change the date of the comment to the early 1880s? The answers are not at all clear.

Indeed, the *Texana* article contains several problems. Williams writes that the first time Quanah Parker denied his father was killed at the Pease River battle "seems to have been made" in a speech at Quanah, Texas, on July 9, 1896. He likewise states that Quanah Parker repeated the denial at the State Fair of Texas in the fall of 1910.[14] Although Williams did not mention it, Quanah Parker's first State Fair denial of his father's death was October 26, 1909, which was the speech that elicited Tom Padgitt's letter to the *Dallas Morning News*.[15]

As to the date of Parker's first denial that Peta Nocona was killed at Pease River, Williams is in error. Charles Goodnight, the Panhandle rancher, reported that "in the winter of 1877 and 1878" Quanah Parker told him Sul Ross killed "Nobah," information Goodnight also got "from old Comanche warriors." Of even greater damage to Williams's assertion concerning the date of Parker's first denial are statements contained in a January 27, 1887, letter Marion T. Brown addressed to her mother while visiting at Fort Sill: "Mr. Jones brought Quanah Parker to see us yesterday. He was in full Indian costume. I will write out what he said, and then read it to Mr. Jones to see if everything is correctly stated. I mean I have written it down. His father was not killed in the battle of Pease River, and lived about five years after the battle. What do you think of that, father?"[16]

From Goodnight's statement and Brown's letter it is obvious Quanah's first denials that his father was killed at Pease River were at least in 1878 or 1887 and not on July 9, 1896. Quanah, it seems logical, would have no reason to deny publicly his father was killed at Mule Creek until 1886, when James DeShields's book with the authorized account appeared saying Ross killed his father. Until then he had no reason to think the general public thought his father was killed in the fight. After all, Ross had claimed in what he described as a "correct history" of the Pease River fight that the chief he killed was Mohee.

Williams's claim—that Quanah Parker's 1896 Quanah, Texas, speech was the first time he had stated Peta Nocona was not killed at the fight—is important. It allows Williams to argue that Quanah's conversation with John Wesley, whether in the early 1880s or the early 1890s, predated any denial by Quanah Parker that his father was killed at Pease River. Nothing in Williams's article indicates he was familiar with either Goodnight's statement or Brown's letter.[17]

As stated earlier, Williams was impressed with Benjamin Gholson's 1931 interview. He uses Gholson's erroneous horse count to support an argument that would give Quanah Parker a reason for changing his story about his father's death. Following Gholson, Williams claims that Peta Nocona was responsible for the loss of 370 horses and mules. He therefore assumes, apparently, that Peta Nocona would have found himself in disgrace among his people.[18] Such a circumstance, the disgrace, would harm the Nocona family, including Quanah, and as a result Quanah began to deny his father's presence at the Mule Creek hunting camp.

Gholson's number of horses is bogus, as are his numbers for Comanches present or killed. Williams did not indicate that he was familiar with the two early Sul Ross accounts, both of which state that about forty horses were taken. Neither does he indicate he was familiar with Sergeant John Spangler's count of forty-five nor the "about thirty"

mentioned in Jonathan Hamilton Baker's diary. If he had been familiar with any of these accounts, Williams would have known there was
little reason for Quanah to defend his father on account of Gholson's
inflated numbers.

Some key arguments in "The Case for Peta Nocona" are based on
alleged statements made by Cynthia Ann Parker through interpreters
and the translations of conversations with Quanah Parker before he
understood English thoroughly. Many of the problems associated with
the translations of both Cynthia Ann Parker's and Quanah Parker's conversations can be traced to the manner in which prereservation Comanches expressed themselves when speaking of family relationships.
The skill and credibility of the translations therefore are paramount to
a fair evaluation of Williams's arguments.

At Mule Creek all of what Sul Ross understood Cynthia Ann Parker
to have said came from his Mexican servant, who acted as interpreter.
Ross claimed the servant had once been a captive of the Comanches
and spoke their language as fluently as his mother tongue. Benjamin
Gholson claimed the servant had been a captive of Peta Nocona and
had been his personal slave. Gholson also claimed the servant told Ross
that the Comanche Ross had confronted was in fact Peta Nocona.[19]
Ross never claimed his servant had been a captive of Peta Nocona or
identified him or even knew him; these allegations all came from Gholson. However, in spite of Ross's silence on the matter, recall that part
of the Chelsey comment that Williams included in his article had to do
with Gholson's claims concerning the prior relationship between the
servant and Nocona. There is no question as to Williams's confidence
in Gholson.

Ross claims he sent his servant with Cynthia Ann Parker to Camp
Cooper to serve as an interpreter. Gholson, however, claims Ben Kiggins acted as interpreter at Camp Cooper. Goodnight disagrees, as
he claims Ross sent word for Kiggins to serve as interpreter at Ross's

permanent camp on Elm Creek, west of Fort Belknap, and not at Camp Cooper. No matter where Ross requested Ben Kiggins to act as an interpreter, why did he make such a request if he had confidence in his servant as an interpreter? Perhaps his faith in his servant was wanting.

Charles Goodnight certainly had an unfavorable impression of the ability of Ross's servant to act as an interpreter. Goodnight said, "We had a Mexican acting as a very poor interpreter. He knew no Comanche and Cynthia knew no English or Spanish." Despite Goodnight's evaluation of the Mexican interpreter or any reservations Ross might have shown about his servant's abilities to act as an interpreter, Robert Williams claimed, "There seems to be no reason to doubt the qualifications of this interpreter."[20]

To the contrary, if Gholson was correct and the Mexican servant told Ross on the battlefield that the warrior Ross fought was Peta Nocona, why did Ross think in the early 1870s that he killed Mohee? Perhaps Ross gave us the answer to that question when in his self-described "correct history" letter published in the June 19, 1875, *Dallas Weekly Herald* he does not mention his Mexican servant's being present when he killed Mohee. In the letter Ross mentioned the servant only once, and that was when he wrote: "At the camp I called up a Mexican who had been raised by the Comanches" and through him gained information from Cynthia Ann Parker. If the servant had participated either as an interpreter or killer of Mohee, why had Ross not introduced him earlier? In all likelihood the answer is that the Mexican servant was not present and did not interpret anything the warrior said during the fight with Ross. Contrary statements by Gholson and James DeShields are both likely the products of DeShields's imagination.[21]

In addition to possible problems with the Mexican servant as a competent interpreter, there is a problem with Williams's own interpretations of Cynthia Ann Parker's statements concerning "two of her boys," or "two of her sons." Williams, who claimed that "lying does not seem to have been dishonorable among the hard-driven Plains Indians, if it served a purpose," accused Quanah of not being truthful when Quanah said he and his brother were not at the battle site. As a basis for the accusation, Williams cites a statement by Ross quoting Cynthia Ann Parker as saying "*two of her boys* were with her when the fight began, and she was distressed by the fear that they had been killed" (italics added).[22] As Naudah had only two sons, Williams argues, Quanah must have been one of the two boys present.

The Ross Family Papers give a slightly different spin on what was said. They contain the following statement: "[Cynthia Ann Parker] replied that *two of her sons* in addition to the infant daughter, were with her when the fight began and she was distressed by the fear that they had been killed" (italics added).[23]

There is a great difference between a parent's birth sons and other children whom the parent may refer to as "my boys." You do not need to be a coach or teacher or parent to refer often to young people who are not your birth children as "my boys." Consider the book titled *The Victors, Eisenhower and His Boys: The Men of World War II*. It is not about Doud and John Eisenhower.[24] Cynthia Ann Parker had only two sons, and perhaps, if they were with her at the battle, she would have said, "my two boys (or sons) were with me when the battle began" and not "two of my boys" or "two of my sons" the latter implying that she had more than two boys or sons, and only two of them were present.

Ross's friend John Henry Brown certainly thought Cynthia Ann Parker's two sons were not with her at Pease River. In the early 1870s letter written by Sul Ross and published in the June 19, 1875, edition of the *Dallas Weekly Herald*, Ross stated, "Two of her sons by an Indian husband were killed in the battle."[25] The Ross statement prompted Brown to write a letter, printed in the same edition of the *Herald*, correcting

Ross. Brown's letter contained the following statement: "General Ross, on reflection, will remember that her Indian husband was killed in the battle, while her sons *were off in their village elsewhere*" (italics added).[26]

When he wrote the 1870s letter, Ross did not think the Indian he had killed was the husband of Cynthia Ann Parker. Had he thought otherwise, he would not have written that two of her sons "by an Indian husband" had died in the fight. Although he erred about the death of Parker's sons, the comment is important. It is not something one would say if the Indian husband and the boys' father had been killed in the battle, especially as Ross, who was making the statement, supposedly killed the husband. The brief sentence is more in keeping with the idea Ross thought Parker's husband to be someone other than the chief he had killed. After all, Ross knew Mohee was not the husband of Naudah (Parker), or perhaps he did not know the name of her husband. Nor at the time did he know that one of her sons was going to be a famous Comanche chief.

Probably the most compelling evidence that Quanah Parker and his brother were not at Pease River is found in a letter by Captain N. G. Evans, the commanding officer at Camp Cooper. On December 26, 1860, Captain Evans wrote to Major W. A. Nichols at Department of Texas headquarters stating that through his interpreter he had learned the captive woman had two children besides her baby Prairie Flower, and they were with the Northern Comanches.[27] Evidently, Cynthia Ann Parker believed her two sons were with Comanche divisions or hunting bands someplace other than Mule Creek. Clearly, Williams was wrong about Parker's two sons being present at Mule Creek on the day of the massacre.

Likewise, there are solid reasons to question Williams's use of Cynthia Ann Parker's "Noconi" statements to support his argument for Peta Nocona's death. Williams writes that Cynthia Ann Parker's repeating "the name Nocona over and over in her intense distress is one of the

John Henry Brown and daughters Clara and Lizzie, ca. 1862. Reprinted by permission of
Dolph Briscoe Center for American History, University of Texas at Austin.

most convincing bits of evidence I have found anywhere that the chief killed by Ross was, as Ross said, Nocona." Williams gets the information from Charles Goodnight by citing the J. Evetts Haley biography of Goodnight. In the Haley book Goodnight is quoted as saying, "The [woman] was in terrible grief. Through sympathy for her, thinking her distress would be the same as that of our women under similar circumstances, I thought I would try to console her. . . . After speaking a few words to her, I turned back to the creek. . . . Her grief was distressing and intense, and I shall never forget the impression it made on me." Goodnight concludes, "I think here Ross got the impression that he had killed her husband, Nocona, as she was saying a great deal about Nocona, meaning however, that she was in the Nocona band of Indians, a word which, as I understand, means to go, ramble, and not make friends."[28]

Based on the Goodnight statements, Williams asserts in his *Texana* article that Cynthia Ann Parker was "moaning [Nocona's] name over and over." Williams asks, "What reason would she have for repeating over and over the name of the small band to which she belonged"? He concludes, "She did repeat the name Nocona over and over in her intense distress."[29] In the summary of his evidence, Williams states, "After the battle she (Cynthia Ann Parker) kept moaning the name Nocona in intense grief," an allegation, like those mentioned above, without foundation. Even a casual reading of the statement reveals that Goodnight did not state that Cynthia Ann Parker "repeated the name Nocona over and over." Goodnight says Parker "was saying a great deal about Nocona," and perhaps Williams took that to mean "over and over." Most people can say a great deal about a person or place without mentioning a name more than once.

Williams then quotes from Gholson's 1931 statement. He admits Gholson was not a witness to any of the events described but argues that Gholson got the account from other Texas Rangers. Gholson claims Parker "wanted to go back where Nocona was killed." After she was carried there, "she got down and paraded around over Nocona a bit," and "they had to force her away."[30]

In his 1928 statement, Gholson also claimed Parker had to be forced to leave the chief's body. But in 1928 Gholson claimed that Parker showed more grief over the body of a young warrior than she did over the bodies of the other Indians, and that was the reason the warrior was not scalped.[31] Other men weighed in on the issue. Hiram Rogers said, "She did not see Nocona's body—that I know of." Peter Robertson wrote that Parker "did not seem to grieve so much over the death of Peta Nocona."[32]

In a summary of the evidence Williams writes, "After the battle [Parker] kept moaning the name of Nocona in intense grief, a natural emotional reaction, if she had just witnessed Nocona's death."[33] The statement appears to be a deduction he made after considering both the Goodnight and Gholson accounts. That is, of course, assuming there was any mention of Parker "moaning the name of Nocona" in either of the accounts. Would not her failure "to grieve so much over the death of Peta Nocona" be an unnatural emotional reaction if in fact her husband had been killed? However, it would perhaps be an appropriate and natural reaction if the Comanche she was not grieving so much over was not Peta Nocona.

It is evident Parker exhibited some grief and concern over the dead man. Most of us have witnessed a woman or man express some degree of grief, however great or slight, over the death of someone other than one's spouse or children, perhaps another family member, a friend, or other valued acquaintance. Perhaps Parker displayed such grief over the death of a family member, friend, or acquaintance.

As to Sul Ross's statement that he killed Peta Nocona, Williams writes, "Ross was specific and clear and never changed his story."[34] One can only assume Williams was not familiar with Ross's "correct history" of the battle in which Ross claims the chief he killed was Mo-hee. John Henry Brown was familiar with Ross's Mohee claim because he read it in the June 19, 1875, edition of the *Dallas Weekly Herald* and included the statement in his book *Indian Wars and Pioneers of Texas*.[35]

Quanah Parker must have read Brown's 1896 book, or had it read to him. Williams quotes Quanah in a letter to Goodnight as saying, "By reference to the account published by John Henry Brown, the acknowl-edged leading historian of Texas, and which was written shortly after the battle, you will see that he states that Ross killed Mo-he-ww."[36] In the quoted portion of the letter, Quanah is writing about Brown's *Indian Wars and Pioneers of Texas*. But in an endnote in the *Texana* article refer-ring to Quanah's reference to the book, Williams admits, "A scanning of Captain Brown's *History of Texas* failed to reveal any such reference."[37] It was the wrong book. By scanning the wrong book, Williams implied Quanah Parker was incorrect.

Williams finds it "highly unlikely that the famous Nocona could just disappear immediately after the battle, with no traders, no reservation Indians, no Indian agencies reporting word of him thereafter, not even of his death."[38] Williams is right, it would be highly unlikely Nocona would just disappear, and he did not. On December 20, 1886, from Fort Sill, Marion Brown wrote her father a letter containing the follow-ing: "Lieut. [Charles J.] Crane says [Horace Jones, the Camp Cooper interpreter] says Peta Nocona, Quanah Parker's father, was not killed in the Battle of Pease River, that he saw him himself a year and a half after the battle, and knows he has only been dead some nine or ten years."[39]

A month later, Brown reaffirmed the story. In what she describes as her very important "Indian Notes from Interpreter H. P. Jones," and dated January 1887, she writes, "The father, who was not a chief as some of the [whites] supposed, was called Puttack Nocona. . . . At the beginning of the war, Camp [Cooper] was abandoned. Col. Leeper, Indian agent at Ft. Cobb, sent for Mr. Jones to come to him and act as interpreter, which he did." She concludes, while Horace Jones was "still [at Fort Cobb] in the Fall of 61 or 62 Puttack Nocona hearing of him and that he had seen and talked with his wife after her capture came to the Ft. to hear from him with his . . . own [ears] the true stories of her capture and learn what had become of her."[40] Again, the evidence does not support Williams's argument.

As Williams notes, Quanah Parker in his 1910 Texas State Fair speech said Peta Nocona was not killed at Pease River. Quanah's voice and command of the English language were described at the time as follows: "His voice was clear and resonant and easily distinct to those even in the rear of the hall, although his words were occasionally broken and difficult to understand."[41] In the speech Quanah stated, "The Texas history says Gen. Ross killed my father. The old Indians tell me that not so. He no kill my father, I want to get that in Texas history straight up. . . . No kill my father; he not there. I want to get it straight here in Texas history. After that, two year, three year maybe, my father sick. I see him die. I want to get that in Texas history straight up."[42]

As stated earlier, the 1910 speech was not the first one Quanah Parker gave at the Texas State Fair. A year earlier his statements were similar to those he gave in 1910:

> I want to make some Texas history straight up. Some say Sul Ross and Rangers kill my father, Peter Nocona. No not so. I be 11 year old when they capture my mother at Mule Creek fight. She with party of Indians hunting buffalo, and Yaqua was in command of that party. My father with another bunch. Yaqua was killed. So old Indians tell me. I know my father so sad my mother gone he get sick here (touching his breast) and I see tear fall from his eye. And he live not long, but die among his people in peace.[43]

Obviously, although both newspapers had Quanah's statements in quotation marks, neither were direct quotes. Quanah likely would not call his father Peter Nocona. In two other newspaper articles that reported Quanah's 1909 State Fair speech the reporters did not claim they were using direct quotes, but gave narratives of the speech. The *Dallas Daily Times Herald* reported:

> Then came Chief Quanah Parker. He corrected history as it is written. Speaking in a clear voice and using English, which was remarkably good, the old Indian, always a friend of the white man and civilization, and now paymaster for the United States at Cash [*sic*], Okla., told of the real death of his father, Nacona [*sic*]. History says that Nacona [*sic*] was killed in the battle of Montieto, or Medicine Bluff, between Hardeman and Cottle counties. Parker said Nacona [*sic*] was not killed there—it was Nacona's [*sic*] brother, and that Nacona [*sic*] died several years later. The old chief talked intelligently and carried conviction.[44]

In January 1910 *The Indian Craftsman*, most likely quoting from the *Dallas Daily Times Herald* article, reported, "At the Texas State Fair at Dallas, Texas, recently, when 'Quanah Route Day' was being celebrated, Chief Quanah Parker, one of the most prominent Indian chiefs in the country and a leading citizen of Oklahoma, was present with his family, and made an address." Quanah "told of the real death of his father, Nacona, [*sic*] who was reported to have been killed in the battle of Montieto, or Medicine Bluff, between Hardeman and Cottle Counties. Parker related that Nacona [*sic*] was not killed at this time, but that it was Nacona's [*sic*] brother. Nacona [*sic*] died several years later."[45]

In his 1928 statement, Benjamin Gholson talked about the captured Comanche boy Sul Ross brought back to Waco and named Pease Ross.

Quanah Parker, ca. 1890. Reprinted by permission of Southwest
Collection/Special Collections Library, Texas Tech University, Lubbock.

After his capture, according to Gholson, the boy threatened the Texas Rangers by telling them what Peta Nocona was going to do to them when he took his revenge. Gholson claimed the boy did not know Nocona had been killed.[46] According to Gholson, Ross's Mexican servant was interpreting all that both Parker and the boy were saying. It is reasonable to assume the captives were kept together in the Ranger camp, as it would be easier to guard them and interpret what they were saying if they were in the same location. Of course, the boy could not understand what the Rangers were saying, even if they had been discussing the death of Peta Nocona. Are we to believe that Parker would not have told the boy about Nocona's death, especially after she heard him threaten the Texas Rangers with Peta Nocona's revenge? If Peta Nocona were alive, Parker would have had no reason to inform the boy that his threats were in vain.

Conversely, perhaps important evidence that Peta Nocona died in the Battle of Pease River is contained in the same letter mentioned above that Captain Nathan Evans on December 26, 1860, wrote to Major W. A. Nichols. In reference to the captured Cynthia Ann Parker, Captain Evans states, "Through the interpreter I learned that she has been a captive for many year [sic] that her husband an Indian was killed in the fight."[47]

Although the interpreter was Horace P. Jones, there is some confusion. Charles Goodnight and Benjamin Gholson both stated Ben Kiggins acted as the interpreter for Cynthia Ann Parker. Goodnight said Kiggins performed this service at Ross's Elm Creek camp, and Gholson said it was done at Camp Cooper. Goodnight's claim has greater merit, for Camp Cooper's post returns for November 1860 through January 1861 list Jones as a scout and interpreter, the same Jones who told Marion Brown he had talked to Peta Nocona at Fort Cobb in either 1861 or 1862.

Moreover, Jones was a superb interpreter. In a letter dated September 22, 1873, General Henry Alvord of East Hampton, Massachusetts, advised Texas Governor E. J. Davis that Jones was one of only two "safe" interpreters in the country, the other being Philip McCuster. According to Alvord, Jones was considered competent, was a master of both languages, and had the confidence of the Indians. With Jones being on the payroll and available, Alvord's praise of the skilled interpreter makes it abundantly clear there was no reason for the military to use the Mexican servant or Kiggins.[48]

Without question the interpreter Evans referred to in his letter to Major Nichols was Horace Jones. This being so, one would think that if Jones thought Peta Nocona had been killed in 1860, upon seeing and talking to Nocona a year or two later it would have made a remarkable impression on him. It seems likely he would have said something to Marion Brown about the surprise of meeting a person he thought had been dead for at least a year, but he did not.

All this being so, what is the meaning of Cynthia Ann Parker's statement about the death of someone she referred to as her husband? Was she referring to Peta Nocona or to someone else? In prereservation Comanche society the custom was for the wife to refer to both her husband and his brothers as her husband. She might have used the Comanche word *kumahpi* or *mukwo* or even *namuwoo* in making the reference. This is not to say the Comanches do not have other words for brother-in-law, for they do. Those words include *puhu te'tsi* or *re'tsi*. However, it is customary for a Comanche woman to use the same word in referring to both her husband and his brothers, and that would be the Comanche word for husband.[49]

To some degree prereservation Comanches practiced the levirate: marriage of a man with his brother's widow. Among the Comanches the custom led to the practice of what was known as anticipatory levirate, in which a husband shared his wife with his younger brothers in a polyandrous household. Such customs may account for a Comanche wife's referring to both her husband and brothers-in-law by the same word. After all, a brother-in-law was her potential husband. Thomas Gladwin, writing in *American Anthropologist*, described for some women an alternate course. He said, "A man's brother's wife, who had always called him 'husband,' and who was potentially his wife through the levirate, might upon the death of this brother start calling him by a sibling term. Such action would indicate that it was not necessary for the man to fulfill his obligation of replacing his brother as her husband."[50]

One cannot know what word Naudah (Parker) used when talking to the Camp Cooper interpreter. What we can be sure of is that she used a Comanche word for husband, which could have been a reference to either her husband or one of his brothers. Since she would have referred to both of them as her husband, could she have been referring to a brother-in-law rather than her husband? Recall that in 1909 Quanah Parker said it was Nocona's brother, Naudah's brother-in-law, who was killed. In Comanche kinship terms, Cynthia Ann Parker would have referred to this brother-in-law as her husband.

Clearly, problems with translating both Cynthia Ann Parker's and Quanah Parker's conversations resulted in misunderstanding and confusion in reference to the Battle of Pease River. In prereservation Comanche society it was customary for a son to refer to both his father and his father's brothers as his father, perhaps using the Comanche word *ahpu'* in doing so. Again, that is not to say the Comanches do not have a word for uncle; it is *ara'*. However, just as having a word for brother-in-law did not keep a prereservation Comanche woman from referring to her husband's brothers as her husband, having a word for uncle did not keep a prereservation Comanche from referring to his uncle as his father. Also, in prereservation society cousins were classified as siblings and referred to as either brother or sister. A Comanche would use the same word, *taka* or *samohpu,* in referring to a brother, sister, or cousin. Such is not to imply the Comanches do not, and did not, have other words that also cover such kin relationships as brother (*samohpu, pabi',* and *tami'*), sister (*samohpu*), or cousin (*haipia'* or *haitsi*).[51]

When he had his alleged conversation with John Wesley in the early 1880s or early 1890s, Quanah Parker was probably using very broken English. There is no indication Wesley spoke the Comanche language. Quanah's English in the early 1890s would have been superior to what it was in the early 1880s, but not as good as it would be in 1909 or 1910. If Wesley spoke Comanche, the conversation was undoubtedly in that language, and the word that Quanah Parker used and Wesley interpreted as father could have been interpreted to mean either "father" or "uncle." The word they interpreted as brother could just as easily have been interpreted as cousin.[52]

If Wesley did not speak the Comanche language, his conversation with Quanah would more than likely have been in English. If this were the case, Quanah would not be expected to have departed from the way his Comanche society viewed and expressed kin relationships. If the Comanche society and custom used the same word to refer to both father and uncle and another word to refer to both cousin and brother, Quanah in the early 1880s or early 1890s would have used the equivalent English words, if he knew them, to refer to such kin.

Quanah's brother was not captured in the Battle of Pease River, nor was his father killed there. Therefore, if Quanah told Wesley his brother was captured, Quanah must have been referring to some kin other than a brother, perhaps a cousin. If he told Wesley his father was killed, he must have been referring to some kin other than his father, whether speaking in Comanche or in English.

Whenever he had his conversation with John Wesley, Quanah Parker probably had no great command of the English language. As late as March 1905 an article appeared describing Parker as he addressed a student assembly at the Carlisle Indian Industrial School in Pennsylvania. The article reported of Quanah: "He speaks English brokenly, can neither read nor write, but is a warm supporter and patron of schools."[53] Apparently because Quanah's English was "broken," he addressed the assembly through Walter Komali, an interpreter.

On a different matter, a Comanche man could have several wives. Quanah Parker had as many as six or seven wives. In a 1911 letter to Charles Goodnight, the letter that prompted Robert Williams to scan the wrong John Henry Brown book, Quanah Parker stated, "My mother [Cynthia] Ann Parker and another of my [father's] wives" were at the Pease River fight. He also notes in the letter that the other wife at Mule Creek died in the fight, and furthermore he writes that when the "fight took place my father with the main body of Indians was about seventy or eighty miles away with his Indian wife my [brother] and myself." According to his own son, therefore, Peta Nocona had at least three wives. If he was a prominent leader of a Comanche hunting band, Nocona could have had additional wives.[54]

To support such a view, consider the following: In his 1928 interview, Ben Gholson reported that, when they were leaving camp, the Texas Rangers allowed Cynthia Ann Parker to claim all the horses and other property belonging to Peta Nocona. Parker refused to take anything, saying Peta Nocona had two more (women or wives) who had the same right to the property that she had. Granted, Gholson cannot be trusted.[55] But as noted in Quanah Parker's letter to Goodnight, one of Peta Nocona's wives was killed in the Pease River fight. If Gholson is correct, then Cynthia Ann Parker, who we are told visited the bodies of all the dead Comanches, would not have included the dead wife in her count of the two wives with whom she should share Peta Nocona's property. If so, Nocona had at least four wives. In any event, consideration of the wives tale seems to mean Peta Nocona had at least three wives and maybe more.

In the summer of 1940, Columbia University, under the direction of George Herzog, sponsored a study in which Comanches were interviewed concerning kin behavior. Based on the study, Thomas Gladwin, in his *American Anthropologist* article entitled "Comanche Kin Behavior," states: "If there were several wives, one was usually considered the favorite, though this was not necessarily the one the man had married first. She did much less work, bossed the household, and was much more intimate with her husband. When traveling, it was she who always carried her husband's shield, while the others tended the pack animals that carried the greasy meat, which would have impaired the husband's power."[56]

What does Gladwin's description of the favored wife tell us about Peta Nocona's relationship with Naudah (Parker)? She was not carrying the shield of the Indian Ross shot. Ross claimed the Indian he shot had his shield covering his back. Of course, according to Gladwin, when the favorite wife was menstruating, the man carried his own shield, and perhaps Naudah was menstruating. On the other hand, perhaps she was one of the "others" who tended the pack animals carrying the greasy meat, and the favored wife was with Peta Nocona in another camp. Goodnight described Parker as having hands that "were extremely dirty from handling so much meat," and Jonathan Baker's diary described a very large amount of meat, skins, and leather bags filled with bison viscera scattered across the prairie.

The "other," or secondary wives, who may have included Naudah, were chore wives. Gladwin's statement that such wives would be "tending the pack animals that carried the greasy meat" fits the party of Comanches Baker writes about in his diary. Quanah Parker's 1911 letter to Goodnight clearly indicates Peta Nocona on December 19, 1860, rode with a favorite wife some eighty miles from the Mule Creek hunting camp, and he had left two of his wives behind, apparently to tend the pack animals that carried the greasy meat. But, frankly, little is known about Naudah's life as a chore wife.

Even less is known about the life of her husband, Peta Nocona.

Robert Williams quoted newspaperman Victor M. Rose as having called him a "great, greasy lazy buck." Sul Ross, perhaps for his own purposes, elevated him to a "noted warrior of great repute." Some authors have called him the head chief of the Noconi Comanches. Others have pointed out his name does not appear on contemporary lists of Comanche leaders or have said he "was not a chief as some of the white [sic] supposed." Most of what little is known of him, oddly enough, centers at the Battle of Pease River, an engagement in which he did not take part. Peta Nocona, however, became known in Texas as the husband of the mythic Cynthia Ann Parker and the father of famed Comanche chief Quanah Parker.

It is the mythic stature of Cynthia Ann Parker and the fame of Quanah Parker that Sul Ross, with help from his political backers, determined to use for political gain. The plan worked, and in part it contributed to Ross's overwhelming election victory in the governor's race in 1886. The myth of Peta Nocona's death along Mule Creek in 1860 is a clear example of how memory, in this case collective memory, is manufactured more than recalled.

Robert Williams, in other words, was wrong about the death of Peta Nocona at the Battle of Pease River. So was Sul Ross, of course, but Ross knew it. Quanah Parker repeatedly denied his father died there. Horace Jones, one of the federal government's most accomplished interpreters, said he saw Peta Nocona at least a year after the battle. And Marion Brown, who about the time of the Ross election campaign visited with Quanah and Jones, wondered, "What will Sul Ross say about Puttack Nocona?" She then added, "I rather enjoy it myself."[57]

# 6

## CONCLUSION
### Explaining the Myths

There are many eyewitness descriptions of the events that occurred on December 19, 1860, near the junction of freshwater, spring-fed Mule Creek and the gypsum-laced Pease River. The most credible of them are Lawrence S. "Sul" Ross's three earliest accounts, Sergeant John W. Spangler's two military reports, and Jonathan H. Baker's original diary. Although they are not identical, these six accounts, when taken together, provide the basic information for constructing a reliable history of the Battle of Pease River and the capture of Cynthia Ann Parker.

In brief, the accounts show that twenty federal troops and not more than twenty Texas Rangers surprised and struck a Comanche hunting village containing nine "grass tents" and approximately fifteen Indians, mostly women and children, who had packed their provisions and were preparing to leave. The Rangers pounded a small group of Indians attempting to escape, and the federal troops rode after a group fleeing in a different direction. From an Anglo point of view, the attack was a success. The Rangers and federal troops captured three Indians, including Cynthia Ann Parker, and killed seven others, four women and three men. About six Indians got away, either because of the cavalrymen's jaded horses or because the troopers were reluctant to kill women and children who were offering no resistance and trying to escape.

In essence, such was the Battle of Pease River. That this tragic killing of women underwent transmutation to a heroic Ross and Ranger victory over a superior force of Comanche warriors can best be explained by politics and a conquering society's inclination toward myth-making.

Sul Ross and his political managers were largely responsible. In the late nineteenth century the shifting Ross versions of the battle and Parker's capture went largely unchallenged. In fact, between his election as governor in 1886 and his death in 1898, Ross controlled the story through his authorized account in James T. DeShields's book *Cynthia Ann Parker.*[1] His descriptions in the lively account gained acceptance and prominence because of his stature: he was a frontier and Civil War hero, a state senator, a popular governor of the state, and later president of Texas A&M College. Indeed, his versions in essence became Texans' collective memory of the paired events. Moreover, his political friends, including especially Victor M. Rose, John Henry Brown, and James DeShields, promoted the mythic Ross versions even if they knew, as did Brown, that the stories were wrong.

The misconceptions, errors, and disregard for truth began early. In fact, as early as 1875, half a century before Araminta McClellan Taulman complained to the editor of *Frontier Times* about errors, Brown saw problems, particularly about who had captured Naudah, the blue-eyed Cynthia Ann Parker. Brown groused about the errors in a column in the *Dallas Weekly Herald.* "History," he argued, "is valuable to mankind only in so far as it is faithfully chronicled."[2]

On the other hand, Brown himself was not immune to exaggeration and hyperbole. In describing the fight at Mule Creek in *Indian Wars and Pioneers of Texas*, he wrote that Ross's men "administered a blow that forever crushed the warlike Comanches" and that Peta Nocona was "the last of the great Comanche chiefs." There were sixty Texas Rangers in the battle, he said, and they captured eight hundred horses.[3] Brown knew better, or should have. Apparently, Brown wrote with the hope of making Ross look as good as possible.

The effort did not always work. At the end of 1886 a copy of James DeShields's book, with its marred authorized account, found its way to Fort Sill on the Comanche Reservation in Indian Territory. Post surgeon Major Morse K. Taylor read it and in December pronounced its author "no writer at all."[4] One does not know if Dr. Taylor was referring to DeShields's prose style or to "facts" presented in the book. Horace Jones, the former Camp Cooper interpreter, who spent a lot of time in the Fort Sill library, probably read the book or heard about it from Taylor. Of the battle along Mule Creek, he said, "Ross gets all or too much glory all the way through the fight."[5]

Although not referring to the book, Jones protested the authorized account. At Fort Sill, he told Marion T. Brown, daughter of Ross's political friend John Henry Brown, "Peta Nocona was not one of the 'big men' among the Indians," and in her notes of the conversation Brown reports Jones as saying that Peta Nocona "was not a chief as some of the [whites] supposed."[6] She also wrote to her father indicating that Jones said, "Peta Nocona . . . was not killed in the Battle of Pease River," and that Jones saw Nocona "a year and a half after the battle."[7] Believing her father might have shared with Sul Ross, who by this time was the governor of Texas, some of the information about Peta Nocona in her letters, she wrote to her mother asking, "What will 'Sul' Ross say about Puttack Nocona? I rather enjoy it myself."[8] In another letter she had concluded, "How the mighty have fallen!"[9]

The names Marion Brown and John Henry Brown appear frequently in the story of the Pease River fight and the capture of Cynthia Ann Parker. John Henry Brown read and corrected the Ross mistake printed in the *Galveston News* and the *Dallas Weekly Herald* in 1875, and Brown was one of the principal sources for DeShields's book that produced the authorized account. As noted, Quanah Parker read, or had read to him, Brown's *Indian Wars and Pioneers of Texas*, a section of which has Ross killing Mohee.[10]

Perhaps of all the historians and other writers who have misrepresented the tragic events of the Battle of Pease River, Brown deserves some sympathy or at least benevolent understanding. One can feel his stress. Brown was a politician who had served in the state legislature and as mayor of both Galveston and Dallas. He was acquainted with Ross, and he knew that Ross in the 1870s claimed the Indian he killed was Mohee. Brown was also familiar with Ross's later claim that the Ranger captain had killed Peta Nocona. He was getting letters from his daughter, however, and they refuted Ross's later claim. What was he to do?

Possibly Brown did what many politicians do. He straddled the fence. In his book *Indian Wars and Pioneers of Texas*, he has two sections, one on the Indian wars and another on pioneers. In the Indian wars section he describes the Battle of Pease River and, following Ross's 1870s claim, states that Ross killed Mohee. As noted in chapter 5, this was the section Quanah Parker referenced in his letter to Charles Goodnight and the section Robert Williams did not find when he "scanned" the wrong book. In the pioneers section Brown's article on Ross states that Peta Nocona was the person killed.[11]

Texas book publisher John Jenkins suggests a different reason for Brown's inconsistency. In *Basic Texas Books* Jenkins indicates that Brown worked on *Indian Wars and Pioneers of Texas* sporadically throughout his career. Such an interrupted writing effort might explain why Brown gave conflicting accounts of the name of the person killed.[12]

Yet Brown's inconsistency and even stronger challenges to the authorized account from Morse Taylor and Horace Jones went unnoticed. J. W. Wilbarger's widely read *Indian Depredations in Texas* in 1889 quoted the authorized account nearly verbatim, and seven years later the pioneers section in Brown's *Indian Wars and Pioneers of Texas* carried forward the preferred Ross story. At the time of Ross's death the authorized account was deeply etched in Texans' collective memory.

Beginning in early 1908, however, a decade after Ross's death, his authorized account began to unravel. That year Major Charles Loeffler, who in 1860 had been a member of the Second U.S. Cavalry regiment, claimed in a newspaper he had been the one who first captured Cynthia Ann Parker. His claim was followed quickly by publication in the *San Antonio Express* of Ross's 1861 official report, an account significantly different from the standard version. Unlike the authorized account, the official report gave the number of Indians—fifteen—that the forty Anglos attacked. It had the chief intentionally dismounting "to sell his life as dearly as possible" rather than being involuntarily pulled from his horse by the fall of a dying girl. It had Lieutenant M. W. Somerville possibly in a situation in which the authorized account had placed Ross. Sometime afterward, the official Ross report disappeared. Could it have been removed from the files to protect Ross and the authorized account?

Then came the 1909 Quanah Parker speech at the Texas State Fair in Dallas. In it, Quanah, although he had said much the same thing to Charles Goodnight in 1877 or 1878, to Marion Brown about 1887, and to a gathering on July 9, 1896, in Quanah, Texas, made the startling and very public announcement that his father had not been killed at Mule Creek. The text of his short speech appeared in several newspapers and dramatically caught people's attention. The Dallas speech brought out the rambling Tom Padgitt letter, published in a 1909 issue of the *Dallas Morning News*. Padgitt's letter was designed to defend the traditional version of events that showed his brother-in-law Sul Ross killing Peta Nocona. The next fall, October 1910, several newspapers reported Quanah Parker's next visit and second speech at the State Fair, one in which he again denied his father's death in December 1860.

Finally, more than half a century after the Battle of Pease River and the 1860 capture of Cynthia Ann Parker, former participants began to get their versions of the conjoined events published. They themselves knew that others at Mule Creek had erred, enhanced their tales, or simply got their stories wrong. And some of them may have believed others presented the story, or changed or embellished battlefield incidents, for personal gain.

Peter Robertson, one of the militiamen, questioned stories about the Pease River incident. He said, for example, that no friendly Indians fought with the Texas Rangers, a reference to the ridiculous statement in Tom Padgitt's 1909 letter in which Padgitt claimed half of Ross's company were friendly Indians. Robertson closed his 1920 remarks with a caution, saying, "I was there, and was an eye-witness to the facts I am relating, and while I have no desire to contradict any other, I would like for the people of Texas to know the facts of history, and not accept the hearsay of any man."[13]

Likewise, Benjamin Dragoo, a Texas Ranger, reported his version in the 1920s. He stated, "There have been many luminous stories told and written about Capt. Ross' capture of Cynthia Ann Parker and his duel with her husband, the big Indian chief." He disagreed with some of the tales, and, like Robertson, he concluded, "My purpose is to give facts in these matters and render honor to whom honor is due. I shall not dispute any man's statement, but will tell it as I saw it."[14] The admonitions, if such they were, suggest Pease River participants kept abreast of accounts of the battle.

What were the former participants reading or hearing that was different from their own recollections? DeShields's book appeared in 1886, and it was followed three years later by Wilbarger's *Indian Depredations in Texas*, which also contained the authorized account. Some other secondary works touching on the Mule Creek incident were in print besides Brown's *Indian Wars and Pioneers of Texas*, which contains conflicting stories: Norman B. Wood's terribly flawed 1906 study, *Lives of Famous Indian Chiefs*, and B. B. Paddock's widely read *A Twentieth-Century History and Biographical Record of North and West Texas* were published in 1906. Each contains misinformation on the Battle of Pease River. In 1912 DeShields published *Border Wars of Texas*, a book in which he eliminated some but not all of his earlier mistakes relating to the battle. In 1914 the *History of the Cattlemen of Texas* appeared, and it included errors about the Pease River events.

Of course other materials were available, some dating to before the authorized account. Could the participants have seen a copy of the 1875 *Galveston News* or *Dallas Weekly Herald*, both of which have a Ross "retelling" that differs from the 1886 authorized account? Could the Ross information contained in such publications have appeared in other newspapers, which was a common practice at the time? Had they seen the 1908 *San Antonio Express* or *Beeville Bee*, which carried Ross's 1861 official report of the fight at Mule Creek? Jonathan Hamilton Baker's diary describing the last days of December 1860 had been written at the time, obviously, but not until about 1911 had portions of it appeared in the *Mineral Wells Index*. Quanah Parker's version in Comanche oral tradition was being circulated at least by the mid-1880s, but Quanah's tale did not go beyond denying his father's death at Mule Creek.[15]

Unfortunately, some of the participants' reports, particularly Benjamin Gholson's two discredited interviews, muddied the story. Indeed, the once conventional story of the Pease River fight and the taking of Naudah from her Comanche family and friends had entered the Texas collective memory largely through lies, myth, and tales constructed from folklore. As a result, the story created problems for judging reliable knowledge about the symbiotic actions. "Reliable history," writes historian Will Bagley, "requires accurate data."[16] In the case of the Battle of Pease River, missing documents, contradictory eyewitness accounts, false memory, and fictionalized diary entries explain in part the difficulty in acquiring accurate data on the event and the absence of reliable histories of what occurred.

Indeed, the problem of what constitutes reliable "truth" and the use of faulty sources has produced misinformation and errors of fact in the secondary accounts and histories of the Mule Creek fight and the capture of Parker. How have twentieth-century historians, biographers, and writers fared in handling the material with all its flaws? Not surprisingly, their studies vary both in quality and in the amount of attention given the events. Some have exhibited skill and care, for they have dug deep in the records.

Others, by relying on questionable accounts while overlooking more accurate sources, too often got the facts wrong. Few authors, for example, used Sergeant John W. Spangler's official reports; Margaret Schmidt Hacker, Jack Selden, and Mike Cox remain the exceptions. As federal troops were involved, one would think the Spangler reports necessary for a solid understanding of the battle. Hacker, Selden, and Rupert N. Richardson are among only a few scholars who used the 1861 *Dallas Herald*, which contains Sul Ross's comments about the engagement just days after it occurred. Even fewer writers used Ross's letter in the 1875 *Dallas Weekly Herald* or *Galveston News*. Many historians, if they used Jonathan Baker's diary, relied on the copy with its fictionalized material rather than the original and then too often used the flawed entries.[17] Only Selden cites the January 4, 1861, Ross report to Governor Sam Houston and Susan Parker St. John's 1894 interview with Ross.

Too many authors used Benjamin Gholson's interviews.[18] But after reading Ross's report to Governor Houston, Spangler's reports, the 1861 *Dallas Herald*, and Baker's original diary, one loses all confidence in Gholson's memory or accuracy. Anyone familiar with such accounts should dismiss Gholson's fantastic claims.

A short review of secondary works touching on the Battle of Pease River and the capture of Cynthia Ann Parker can be divided into several categories. Such divisions include biographies of Cynthia Ann Parker, Quanah Parker, and Sul Ross, of course, plus histories of the Texas Rangers. They also encompass regional works, county histories, and military studies, including Indian raids and state and federal troop operations. State histories represent still another category, but most of them, as with nearly all histories of the Comanches, give very little attention to the massacre. Still, as the number of such books and articles is very large, there is some value to reviewing a representative cross-section of them to illustrate how modern historians and biographers handle the information.

Among the many Cynthia Ann Parker biographies and Parker family histories are some that demonstrate good research and a solid understanding of the fight at Pease River. Margaret Schmidt Hacker's *Cynthia Ann Parker: The Life and the Legend* is one of the better studies. Although she got the date of the battle wrong, Hacker produced an otherwise fine work.[19] Jack K. Selden's *Return: The Parker Story* has the date of the battle correct and provides new information in the form of Sergeant John Spangler's second report to Captain Nathan G. Evans. It is a good, reliable study and thoroughly researched.

Quanah Parker biographies are numerous, some twenty or more.[20]

The best and most reliable is William T. Hagan's *Quanah Parker, Comanche Chief*. Unfortunately, Hagan calls Peta Nocona "a prominent war chief" and writes that Quanah was in the hunting camp at Mule Creek. On the other hand, he claims that Sul Ross did not kill Peta Nocona, for he writes that Horace Jones, the highly respected Fort Sill interpreter, had talked in 1868 with Quanah about the leader's father.[21]

In the major biographies of Sul Ross none of the authors cover the Pease River fight effectively. They either simply repeat the authorized account, which is understandable, as they are writing about Ross, or rely too heavily on other questionable sources, such as the flawed copy of Jonathan Baker's diary and the Gholson interviews.[22]

Many histories of the Texas Rangers mention the Pease River fight. An exception is Walter Prescott Webb's old standard, *The Texas Rangers: A Century of Frontier Defense*, which contains not a word about it. As to the coverage of others, not surprisingly they vary both in quality and in the sweep of attention given to the 1860 fight and Parker's capture. Some Ranger histories contain only minor problems.[23] In some the errors or questionable use of sources are more serious and frequent.[24]

Military histories and general studies of Indian-white conflict in Texas are as numerous as Texas Ranger studies. Among their authors, one of the few historians who defends Indian actions, minimizes Indian raiding, and conversely places most responsibility for Anglo-Indian antagonism on whites, including federal troops, Texas Rangers, and local thugs who disguised themselves as Indians, is Gary Clayton Anderson. His highly acclaimed *The Conquest of Texas: Ethnic Cleansing in the Promised Land, 1820–1875* represents a thorough approach to the subject, but its portrayal of the Battle of Pease River contains information that differs from many of the eyewitness accounts.

Anderson calls Ross's servant a black slave, while nearly every participant's description, including Ross's own reports, refers to the man as a Mexican. Some give his name as Antonio "Anton" Martinez and describe him as a cook. Although Anderson correctly points out that Cynthia Ann Parker's existence among Comanches was well known on the frontier, his related argument that her husband Peta Nocona "was nearly as celebrated" is difficult to substantiate from the evidence. Peta Nocona's "fame," such as it was, grew after his death, after the rise of his son Quanah to prominence, and after Sul Ross used Peta Nocona's life and death to promote his own political career.[25]

In a much earlier account, *Robert E. Lee in Texas*, Carl Coke Rister writes that "a large raiding party of Naconi [*sic*] Comanches, under their great chief, Peta Nacona [*sic*]," had struck the settlements. Rister says Sergeant John Spangler led only thirteen men and that Sul Ross fought "a spirited duel" with Peta Nocona. He is among those scholars who support a post–Civil War death for Cynthia Ann Parker, writing, "Her child, Topasannah [*sic*], or 'Prairie Flower,' died in 1864; and a few years after the Civil War the mother followed her to the grave."[26]

Like Rister, James R. Arnold comments about Peta Nocona's abilities. In *Jeff Davis's Own: Cavalry, Comanches, and the Battle for the Texas Frontier*, Arnold calls him the "much-feared Comanche chief Peta Nocona." Peta Nocona, one should recall yet again, did not become known until after Sul Ross in the early 1880s took political advantage of Quanah Parker's growing fame to describe Nocona as a "noted warrior of great repute." Arnold gives the incorrect December 18 date for the fight, mentions the defensive circle the Comanches formed, and writes that Ross's "command killed fourteen people [and] captured three warriors and several women."

Gregory F. Michno, *Encyclopedia of Indian Wars: Western Battles and Skirmishes 1850–1890*, uses only secondary sources, including Wilbarger's (and thus DeShields's) 1889 study for his description of the fight. Michno writes that about twenty-five warriors were packing up to leave, Parker was riding double behind Peta Nocona, and their son, Quanah, was present but managed to escape. The short piece contains too many errors to be useful, but it offers another example of how the misconceptions and myth associated with the Mule Creek fight have been repeated.

In *Crimson Desert: Indian Wars of the American Southwest*, Odie B. Faulk likewise includes too many errors. He describes the Noconi camp as "large," for example; gives the date of the fight as December 1859 (a printing error, apparently); says "a number of hand-to-hand encounters occurred"; and calls Peta Nocona "Chief." He gives no citation to sources.[27]

Rupert Norval Richardson in *The Frontier of Northwest Texas, 1846–1876* writes about the Pease River incident, calling the Comanche hunting party at Mule Creek "a relatively weak Indian aggregation" and saying the "band was annihilated." He gives the correct date for the surprise attack: December 19, 1860. In a footnote, Richardson writes about Cynthia Ann Parker. "Of her capture," he says, "the best account is the one first written, published in the *Dallas Herald*, Jan. 2, 1860." He meant, of course, 1861.[28]

In the secondary literature, the most thorough discussion of the Battle of Pease River is Joseph Carroll McConnell's *The West Texas Frontier*, but it is not necessarily the best. To his credit McConnell interviewed a number of people in Northwest Texas who were living at the time of the battle, and he examined Charles Goodnight's recollections and a part of Jonathan Baker's diary as printed in the 1911 *Mineral Wells Index*. He also used both the authorized account and John Henry Brown's *Indian Wars and Pioneers of Texas*. He has the date of the battle correct and does not make a decision on the name of the person Ross allegedly killed, but his description of the battle and the capture of Parker largely follow Benjamin Gholson's interviews.

Ida Lasater Huckabay's history, *Ninety-four Years in Jack County*, largely repeats the story as McConnell tells it. There are errors: She has Albert Sidney Johnston commanding Camp Cooper at the time of the fight, and she says the Ross command killed twenty-five or more Indians. She insists that Sul Ross did not kill Peta Nocona, but he fought with "a big Indian," who sang his death song as Ross's Mexican servant shot him. She has Lieutenant Tom Kelliher, rather than one of the federal troops, catching Parker and Ross recognizing her as a white woman but not as Cynthia Ann Parker.[29]

Doyle Marshall writes carefully about Indian raids and white counterattacks. His study, *A Cry Unheard: The Story of Indian Attacks in and around Parker County, Texas, 1858–1872*, is based primarily on secondary sources, but he uses Jonathan H. Baker's diary and Charles Goodnight's recollections for the Pease River fight. And he gets the story correct. Marshall notes that Texas Rangers and federal troops struck "a small Comanche camp of mostly women who were preparing to move their camp to a distant location. In the brief confrontation, soon to be touted to the Texas public as 'The Battle of Pease River,' a few Comanches, mostly women, were killed."

Another competent history is Ty Cashion's *A Texas Frontier: The Clear Fork Country and Fort Griffin, 1849–1887*. The award-winning book is a well-written, thorough discussion of the Fort Griffin, Albany, and Clear Fork country. The Battle of Pease River gets only a paragraph, mainly on Cynthia Ann Parker, and Cashion used Wilbarger, and thus the authorized account, and Joseph Carroll McConnell's *The West Texas Frontier* as his main sources.

Most Comanche histories give little attention to the battle along Mule Creek. Thomas W. Kavanagh, for example, in his nearly six-hundred-page book *Comanche Political History: An Ethnohistorical Perspective, 1706–1875*, writes only: "In December another party of Rangers attacked a Comanche village on the Pease River in Texas, capturing Cynthia Ann Parker."[30] Ernest Wallace and E. Adamson Hoebel in *The Comanches: Lords of the South Plains* mention Cynthia Ann Parker only in a footnote, and they do not write about the battle. Pekka Hämäläinen in his masterful *The Comanche Empire* calls Peta Nocona a "chief," but he does not discuss the massacre along Mule Creek.

Likewise, Gerald Betty in *Comanche Society before the Reservation* writes little about the massacre. He has the date of the battle wrong. Yet with perception missing in most studies of Cynthia Ann Parker and the Mule Creek fight, he notes, "Cynthia Ann eventually married a Comanche chief by the name Peta Nocona, although there is little documentary evidence of the existence of a person by that name."[31]

Rupert N. Richardson in his highly acclaimed *Comanche Barrier to South Plains Settlement* writes only, "Captain L. S. Ross with a small ranger and cavalry force was more successful, attacking a Comanche village on Pease river in the present Foard county, killing and scattering the band and capturing the celebrated Cynthia Ann Parker." Writing in 1933, just as many of the participants' accounts began to appear, Richardson nonetheless notes that Parker's "story is one of the most widely known in all the saga of the Texas frontier."[32]

Stanley Noyes in *Los Comanches: The Horse People, 1751–1845* includes two paragraphs on Parker in the epilogue of his history. Regrettably, his sources include the DeShields book and Bill Neeley's *Quanah Parker and His People*, a novelized biography of the Comanche leader. Noyes writes incorrectly that Naudah's "husband, Peta Nocona, or 'He-Who-Travels-Alone-and-Returns,' was the head chief of the Nokoni Comanches." He also notes, as several other writers do, that Parker died in 1864. As indicated by the 1870 Anderson County, Texas, census, her death more likely occurred after 1870.[33]

In *Comanches: The Destruction of a People*, T. R. Fehrenbach makes several questionable statements. He describes Peta Nocona as a war chief, says the federal troops from Camp Cooper placed "themselves under the state officer's command," and writes that the fight occurred on December 17, 1860. He also notes that the camp "held only women and children and a Mexican male slave." The slave, he writes, "who was trying to save the fleeing Comanche women," is the person Ross killed. His date of the fight is an error, and his claim that experienced federal troopers placed themselves under the command of a twenty-two-year-old Texas Ranger is questionable; Spangler's reports clearly say differently. Fehrenbach argues that Nawkohnee, as he calls Peta Nocona, "never took another woman." Maybe so, but at the time, Peta Nocona already was married to at least two other women.[34]

Comanche oral tradition related to the Battle of Pease River came mainly through Quanah Parker and his daughters, Neda Parker Birdsong and Mrs. Emmett Cox. But, as has been clearly shown, Quanah was not present at the Mule Creek camp. Nonetheless, according to the women, Quanah "forbade his people to tell the truth about the matter." Birdsong, a Carlisle graduate, reported Quanah as saying, "Out of respect to the family of General Ross, do not deny that he killed Peta Nokoni. If he felt that it was any credit to him to have killed my father, let his people continue to believe that he did so."[35] Although he may in fact have so admonished his family, Quanah himself on several occasions, beginning at least by 1878, denied Ross had killed his father.

In some major ways, Comanche oral tradition confirms the positions taken in this book: Sul Ross did not kill Peta Nocona, for example, and neither Nocona nor Quanah were present at the battle. The village was a small hunting camp occupied by women and a few men who were helpers—Mexican slaves, the oral histories call them. There was no battle, but the event "was in reality a massacre of defenseless women. . . . There were no Comanche warriors present."[36]

Conversely, Comanche oral history argues that Peta Nocona married only one woman: Naudah (Cynthia Ann Parker). Archival research suggests that he had at least three wives, a common practice among prominent warriors in mid-nineteenth-century Comanche life. If Comanche oral tradition is correct, Sul Ross killed a Mexican named "Joe (Jose) Nokoni . . . who was owned by Peta Nokoni and was Cynthia

Ann's personal servant." Once the Texas Rangers began "shooting and the Mexican was hit and disabled," the oral history maintains, he at once "began to sing his death song in Comanche, and turning around made a 'dare ride' . . . hoping to stand the Rangers off and enable the women and children to escape." According to Neda Parker Birdsong, "During this single-handed charge, he was shot and killed by Captain Ross." Also according to Birdsong, "One of the captured squaws volunteered the information that [the dead person] was Joe Nokoni . . . and struck by the bravery of this man, Ross came to the conclusion that he had killed the Comanche leader." And, in addition, Birdsong, supported by her sister, said, "Cynthia Ann Parker and her baby, together with several other women and children, were captured immediately afterward."[37]

Clearly, in its version of the Pease River fight Comanche oral tradition contains issues as troublesome as Anglo Texans' collective memory. White soldiers took only three prisoners: Cynthia Ann Parker, her baby daughter, and Pease Ross. Because Comanches did not return to the massacre site to search for their missing loved ones, perhaps the claim that "several other women and children were captured immediately afterward" grew from a wish that the missing people had been captured instead of being killed. If they had returned a few weeks or months later, the Comanches would have found the remains, and their oral history may have been different. Apparently they did not return, for a Thomas Harrison company of Rangers during the spring of 1861 visited the former battleground and noticed that the "skulls and bones were still there."[38] Also, because during the massacre most Comanches were fleeing or dead, only the captives could have witnessed Ross or someone else shooting the Mexican defender or alleged chief. None of them returned to Comanche society to explain the man's death or the death song issue. In the case of the man's demise, then, Comanche oral tradition necessarily comes from non-Indian sources, and DeShields's biography of Parker seems the logical place.

Most modern histories of Texas give very little attention to the Pease River fight or the capture of Parker. Robert Calvert, Arnoldo De Leon, and Gregg Cantrell in *The History of Texas*, for example, do not mention either event, but they indicate that Parker was taken in a Comanche raid in 1836. Likewise, in the ninth edition of their venerable *Texas: The Lone Star State*, Rupert N. Richardson, Adrian Anderson, Cary D. Wintz, and Ernest Wallace write only, "In one of the raids, Comanches took one of their most famous captives, Cynthia Ann Parker, who subsequently married a Comanche chief." Jesus F. de la Teja, Paula Marks, and Ron Tyler in *Texas, Crossroads of North America: A History* write no more than that Sul Ross "was the person who had brought Cynthia Ann Parker back (albeit unwillingly) from Comanche captivity in 1860."

Randolph B. Campbell in *Gone to Texas: A History of the Lone Star State* gives a bit more space to the fight than do some of his colleagues. Among other things, he writes that the "force of about forty Rangers and twenty-one soldiers provided by the U.S. Second Cavalry surprised a party of Comanches on December 19 as they were breaking camp near the Pease River, killing some [people] and scattering the rest."[39] Campbell gets most of the story correct, including the date of the fight, but fewer than twenty Rangers charged the village, and he allows the impression that Sul Ross was in overall command of the expedition. The federal troops probably did not see Ross as their commander.

T. R. Fehrenbach's *Lone Star: A History of Texas and the Texans* is much like his 1974 Comanche book cited previously, at least regarding the Pease River fight. In both the same errors appear—the date and the number of Texas Rangers in Sul Ross's command, for example—but in this history Fehrenbach gives a name, Joe, to the Mexican slave, the person who became Peta Nocona. The Mexican slave part is an argument straight from Comanche oral tradition. Apparently using Charles Goodnight's recollections as a source, Fehrenbach writes that Goodnight first recognized Cynthia Ann Parker as white.[40]

Most shorter histories of the state do not mention the Mule Creek fight or Cynthia Ann Parker. Such is the case with *Texas: A History* and *Texas: All Hail the Mighty State* by, respectively, Joe B. Frantz and Archie P. McDonald. A much larger work, *Texas: A Sesquicentennial Celebration*, edited by Donald W. Whisenhunt and with each of its twenty chapters written by a different Texas historian, also does not include coverage of the battle or Parker. David G. McComb in *Texas: A Modern History* gives some space to Parker, but hardly describes the fight at Mule Creek. Enough authors, including McComb, give 1864 as the year of Parker's death that one wants to believe it is the right date.

Two older histories, Ernest Wallace's *Texas in Turmoil*, a volume in *The Saga of Texas* series, and Seymour V. Connor's *Texas: A History*, cover the battle in more detail. Wallace writes that the expedition "surprised and destroyed a large Nokoni Comanche camp and captured Cynthia Ann Parker, who . . . had become the wife of Chief Peta Nocona. During the fight a number of hand-to-hand encounters occurred, one between Ross and an Indian believed to have been Peta Nocona." The Indian died, but Wallace writes, "Many years later Quanah Parker . . . stated that the man Ross killed was not [Nocona]."[41] Connor writes more and with some of the same questionable information. Like Wallace, he also writes that a "large Nokoni camp was destroyed . . . [and Cynthia Ann Parker] married Chief Peta Nocona."[42]

As has been noted, several authors relied on secondary sources in presenting their version of the fight at Pease River. Many years ago the great transcendentalist Henry David Thoreau gave some good advice about those who were only travelers, as he called them. The advice could apply as well to authors who use only secondary sources. Thoreau wrote, "He who is only a traveler learns things at second-hand and by the halves, and is poor authority."[43] What some authors learned second-hand and by the halves concerning the fight at Pease River and the capture of Cynthia Ann Parker made them poor authorities for both events. Yet, regrettably, what they wrote still contributes to the perpetuation of the myth that has helped construct our collective memory of the storied events.

In the end, although some uncertainty about the Battle of Pease River remains, a few things at least seem clear. Sul Ross altered his accounts of the fight. The temporary little village Captain Ross, Sergeant Spangler, and their fewer than forty men charged was a Comanche hunting camp with only a few men and several women and children present. The fight was brief, lasting just over twenty minutes. After the engagement, during a two-day search, Jonathan H. Baker, the diarist in Jack Cureton's company, and his group found only seven dead bodies on the extended battle site: four women and three men. The Ross-Spangler command took three prisoners, and the massacre, which in our histories soon became a great battle, made Ross a popular hero.

Sul Ross and his influential friends controlled the early histories of the massacre and embellished them to Ross's political benefit. By 1886 they had produced what they saw as the authorized account, a story that would enhance the vote for Ross during the 1886 election for governor. The popular Ross, in fact, received 78 percent of the vote in November, and the approved story quickly became the standard history of the Battle of Pease River.

Benjamin F. Gholson was most assuredly not at Mule Creek. His accounts of the massacre are mostly fiction and entertaining. But even if he was present and his name was on the muster roll, Gholson's stories so conflict with those of known participants as to render his tales worthless for serious consideration. Harvey Chelsey's claim that

Gholson had "a remarkable memory and a high reputation for accuracy" notwithstanding, the evidence shows otherwise concerning his memory, and his reputation for accuracy was not deserved.

Gholson was a good storyteller. He made heroes out of the Texas Rangers and citizen militiamen who were involved in a massacre. Historiographically, the problem is not so much whether Gholson was at the Mule Creek fight. In the final analysis, his presence does not matter. The problem is with otherwise competent writers who have used his fiction as fact. The friendly, talkative, eighty-seven-year-old Gholson cannot be blamed for composing an interesting story to entertain family, amuse friends, and bamboozle interviewers.

Robert H. Williams was wrong about Quanah Parker. Quanah was not in the hunting camp at the time of the attack. On numerous occasions, starting as early as the winter of 1877–78 and continuing until the year before he died in 1911, Quanah said his father was not killed at Pease River, but instead lived a few years after the incident. Williams made much of the fact that Quanah's statements, saying his father was not killed during the Pease River fight, were made several years after the battle and thus Quanah was lying. Williams, unfortunately, labored under the misassumption that Ross had always claimed he had fought Peta Nocona and had never said the person he killed was Mohee. Williams overlooked the fact that it was not until the mid-1880s that Ross changed the name of the person from Mohee to Peta Nocona. Until that time Quanah would have had no reason to believe Ross or anyone else said he killed Peta Nocona, and until the mid-1880s Ross in fact did not say he did. Thus, of course, Quanah had no reason until the 1880s to refute the nonstatement. Quanah denied the claim of his father's death at Mule Creek as soon as he was aware of the falsehood.

Williams was also wrong about Peta Nocona. The clear and convincing evidence shows Peta Nocona was not at the Pease River fight, and Sul Ross probably had no idea of the name of the Comanche man he

Historical marker erected in 1936 for the Battle of Pease River, with
the wrong date. Photograph courtesy of Monte L. Monroe.

fought, and maybe killed, on December 19, 1860. The much-cited but troublesome legal brief Williams prepared arguing for Peta Nocona's death needs revision.

One lesson from Mule Creek is firm: In the collective memory of Texans, the 1860 massacre near Pease River became a major battle in which Comanche hegemony was destroyed, Cynthia Ann Parker at long last was returned to Anglo civilization, and Texas Rangers earned a great victory over a superior force of Comanche warriors. Despite ample evidence to the contrary, such myth and folklore persist.

Scholars are not immune from the mythmaking. The description of Peta Nocona as a Comanche chief, for example, has been repeated since Sul Ross and his cronies in 1886 first wrote such fiction for political purposes. What evidence, besides repetition, establishes Peta Nocona—Puttack—as a chief? Those contemporaries, such as scout Horace Jones, who knew Peta Nocona, denied he was even a "big man" among the Comanches, and Charles Goodnight, who knew Quanah Parker, Nocona's son, claimed that Peta Nocona was not a chief.

Moreover, about the Battle of Pease River and the capture of Naudah, what contemporary information is reliable, and how can one know it is reliable? For political reasons Sul Ross changed his story in the 1870s and again in the 1880s, each time giving himself a greater role in the tragedy. Benjamin Gholson, who was nowhere near Mule Creek, fabricated his tales of the event. Charles Goodnight bent his story in ways to protect the good standing of the Texas Rangers. Hiram Rogers and Ben Dragoo both admitted their memories of the fight that had occurred over half a century earlier were defective. Francis Peveler, a member of Jack Cureton's militia force, did not participate in the actual fight and consequently did not see what transpired during the attack. As to the copy of the Baker diary that many people use, someone other than Baker produced the typed document after the fact with a number of omissions and some erroneous additions. John Spangler, possibly because Ross's report to Governor Sam Houston mentioned only three troopers as being in the fight, provided a second and revised account of the battle.

And, finally, in the larger story of Anglo-Indian conflict in Texas the so-called Battle of Pease River was not particularly significant. Indeed, its importance, such as it is, centers mainly on its use as a lesson in historiography, folklore, and mythmaking. The brief fight along Mule Creek demonstrates again how folklore and collective memory remain difficult to alter. If, in fact, memory is constructed, then collective memory is the handiwork of numerous and varied laborers, and numbers and variety do not make it any more reliable.

# NOTES

## Chapter 1

1. B. A. Botkin, "American Folklore (1949)," in *Folk Nation: Folklore in the Creation of American Traditions*, ed. Simon J. Bronner, 136; Tom Crum, "Is It Folklore or History? The Answer May Be Important," in *Folklore: In All of Us, In All We Do*, ed. Kenneth L. Untiedt, 2–11. See also James E. Crisp, *Sleuthing the Alamo: Davy Crockett's Last Stand and Other Mysteries of the Texas Revolution*, 117, 178.

2. Sandra L. Myres, "Cowboys and Southern Belles," in *Texas Myths*, ed. Robert F. O'Connor, 122–23; Walter L. Buenger and Robert A. Calvert, *Texas Through Time: Evolving Interpretations*, ix–xii. See also Gregg Cantrell and Elizabeth Hayes Turner, eds., *Lone Star Pasts: Memory and History in Texas*.

3. Araminta McClellan Taulman, "The Capture of Cynthia Ann Parker," *Frontier Times* 6, no. 8 (May 1929): 311.

4. Hiram B. Rogers, "Recollections of Ranger H. B. Rogers of the Capture of Cynthia Ann Parker," as told to J. A. Rickard, n.d., filed with "Recollections of B. F. Gholson," as told to J. A. Rickard, August 1928, typescript, Dolph Briscoe Center for American History, University of Texas at Austin.

5. See, for example, John W. Spangler, First Sergeant, Company H, to Nathan G.

Evans, Captain, Second Cavalry, Camp Cooper, December 24, 1860, NA, photocopy in possession of authors; "From the Frontier," *Dallas Herald*, January 2, 1861; Captain L. S. Ross to Governor Sam Houston, January 4, 1861, as it appeared in "More about the Capture of Woman Prisoner," *San Antonio Express*, February 23, 1908, and in "Cynthia Ann Parker Again," *Beeville Bee*, February 28, 1908. A copy of the report is also in Eric C. Caren, comp., *Texas Extra: A Newspaper History of the Lone Star State, 1835–1935*, 103. See also "Indian News," *Galveston Civilian*, January 15, 1861.

6. Paul I. Wellman, "Cynthia Ann Parker," *Chronicles of Oklahoma* 12, no. 2 (June 1932): 163–70.

7. Benjamin F. Gholson interview with Felix Williams and Harvey Chelsey, August 26, 1931, in Rupert N. Richardson, ed., "The Death of Nocona and the Recovery of Cynthia Ann Parker," *Southwestern Historical Quarterly* 46 (July 1942): 17 (hereafter cited as Gholson interview, 1931). For other large numbers of Comanches, see Benjamin F. Gholson, "Recollections of B. F. Gholson," as told to J. A. Rickard, August 1928, typescript, Dolph Briscoe Center for American History, University of Texas at Austin (hereafter cited as Gholson, "Recollections," 1928); James T. DeShields, *Cynthia Ann Parker*, 66.

8. "The Parker Captives," *Galveston News*, June 3, 1875; "The Parker Captives," *Dallas Weekly Herald*, June 19, 1875. For the December 19 date, see "From the Frontier," *Dallas Herald*, January 2, 1861; Ross to Houston, January 4, 1861; U.S. Department of War, Returns from United States Military Posts, 1800–1916, Camp Cooper, December 1860, Roll 253, Microfilm Copy M-617, RG94, NA; Spangler to Evans, December 24, 1860, and John W. Spangler to Nathan Evans, January 16, 1861, in the *San Antonio Ledger*, February 2, 1861, as cited in Jack K. Selden, *Return: The Parker Story*, 292–94.

9. Gholson, "Recollections," 1928, 3–29; Gholson interview, 1931, 15–21.

10. "Quanah Parker Sets History Straight," *Semi-Weekly Farm News* (Dallas), October 29, 1909; "Straightens Out History," *Dallas Morning News*, October 25, 1910.

11. David Thelen, ed., *Memory and American History*, ix, xi.

12. For a more thorough discussion of Comanche military and economic troubles in the 1850s, see Pekka Hämäläinen, *The Comanche Empire*, 292–313.

13. Gary Clayton Anderson, *The Conquest of Texas: Ethnic Cleansing in the Promised Land, 1820–1875*, 9–10, 12, 307, 330–33.

14. Rupert Norval Richardson, *Comanche Barrier to South Plains Settlement*, 108–109; Judith Ann Benner, *Sul Ross: Soldier, Statesman, Educator*, 23; and Kenneth F. Neighbours, *Indian Exodus: Texan Indian Affairs, 1835–1959*, 98.

15. Ida Lasater Huckabay, *Ninety-four Years in Jack County, 1854–1948*, 35–37; Hilory G. Bedford, *Texas Indian Troubles: The Most Thrilling Events in the History of Texas*, 166–68; and Anderson, *Conquest of Texas*, 307.

16. Richardson, *Comanche Barrier*, 119–21; W. J. Hughes, *Rebellious Ranger: Rip Ford and the Old Southwest*, 134–48; Anderson, *Conquest of Texas*, 304–307; Huckabay, *Ninety-four Years in Jack County*, 40–45; Stan Hoig, *Tribal Wars on the Southern Plains*, 170–71; Thomas W. Kavanagh, *Comanche Political History: An Ethnohistorical Perspective, 1706–1875*, 365–67; Thomas T. Smith, *The Old Army in Texas: A Research Guide to the U.S. Army in Nineteenth-Century Texas*, 144.

17. Benner, *Sul Ross*, 23–25; Hoig, *Tribal Wars of the Southern Plains*, 177–78; Harold B. Simpson, *Cry Comanche: The 2nd U. S. Cavalry in Texas, 1855–1861*, 107, 109–11.

18. Kavanagh, *Comanche Political History*, 375; W. S. Nye, *Carbine and Lance: The Story of Old Fort Sill*, 22; Richardson, *Comanche Barrier*, 121; and Smith, *Old Army in Texas*, 145.

19. Kavanagh, *Comanche Political History*, 375.

20. Hoig, *Tribal Wars*, 179. See also Anderson, *Conquest of Texas*, 310–11; Benner, *Sul Ross*, 28–30; Nye, *Carbine and Lance*, 18–23; Richardson, *Comanche Barrier*, 121–22; Simpson, *Cry Comanche*, 108–112; Kavanagh, *Comanche Political History*, 375; and Hämäläinen, *Comanche Empire*, 311.

21. Benner, *Sul Ross*, 32–33, 33n33; Simpson, *Cry Comanche*, 117.

22. Richardson, *Comanche Barrier*, 123–25; Benner, *Sul Ross*, 36–37; Anderson, *Conquest of Texas*, 312–17; Kavanagh, *Comanche Political History*, 375, 379–81.

23. Benner, *Sul Ross*, 38.

24. Ibid., 45. See also Anderson, *Conquest of Texas*, 330–31.

25. L. S. Ross to Governor Sam Houston, September 18, 1860, Governor's Papers, Sam Houston Correspondence, Texas State Archives, Austin; Benner, *Sul Ross*, 47–48.

26. Doyle Marshall, *A Cry Unheard: The Story of Indian Attacks in and around Parker County, Texas, 1858–1872*, 29–35; Huckabay, *Ninety-four Years in Jack County*, 60–64; John Carroll McConnell, *West Texas Frontier*, 26–32.

27. Rupert Norval Richardson, *The Frontier of Northwest Texas, 1846–1876*, 210–11; McConnell, *West Texas Frontier*, 32–33; Marshall, *A Cry Unheard*, 39–45.

28. Benner, *Sul Ross*, 50–51; McConnell, *West Texas Frontier*, 32–33; Marshall, *A Cry Unheard*, 43–44; Simpson, *Cry Comanche*, 153; Smith, *Old Army in Texas*, 147.

29. J. Evetts Haley, ed., "Charles Goodnight's Indian Recollections," *Panhandle-Plains Historical Review* 1 (1928): 20.

30. Spangler to Evans, January 16, 1861.

31. "From the Frontier," *Dallas Herald*, January 2, 1861; Ross to Houston, January 4, 1861; Spangler to Evans, December 24, 1860; and Jonathan Hamilton Baker, Diary of Jonathan Hamilton Baker, manuscript, entry for December 20, 1860, private collection, Tarrant County Historical Commission, Fort Worth (hereafter cited as Baker, Diary—first, manuscript). See also, Jonathan Hamilton Baker, Diary of Jonathan [James] Hamilton Baker, 1858–1918, typescript, Dolph Briscoe Center for American History, University of Texas at Austin.

32. United States Federal Census, Ninth Census, 1870, Palestine, Texas, Schedule I—Inhabitants of Anderson County, Texas, p. 212. See also Selden, *Return*, 208n***.

33. Baker, Diary—first, manuscript, entry for December 19, 1860. Several different versions of post-fight developments are available. See, for example, Benner, *Sul Ross*, 54–57; Selden, *Return*, 170–75; and Anderson, *Conquest of Texas*, 332.

## Chapter 2

1. For a larger discussion of folklore, history, and collective memory, see Tom Crum, "Is It Folklore or History? The Answer May Be Important," in *Folklore: In All of Us, In All We Do*, ed. Kenneth L. Untiedt, 3–11, and Gregg Cantrell and Elizabeth Hayes Turner, eds. *Lone Star Pasts: Memory and History in Texas*. The Abernethy definition is in F. E. Abernethy, "Classroom Definition of Folklore," in *Between the Cracks of History: Essays on Teaching and Illustrating Folklore*, ed. F. E. Abernethy, 4.

2. James T. DeShields, *Cynthia Ann Parker*, 41–44. See also J. W. Wilbarger, *Indian Depredations in Texas*, 335–38.

# NOTES

3. Hiram B. Rogers, "Recollections of Ranger H. B. Rogers of the Capture of Cynthia Ann Parker," as told to J. A. Rickard, n.d., filed with Benjamin Franklin Gholson, "Recollections of B. F. Gholson," as told to J. A. Rickard, August 1928, in Dolph Briscoe Center for American History, University of Texas at Austin.

4. Ibid.

5. "Ben Dragoo Tells of the Capture of Cynthia Ann Parker," *Frontier Times* 1, no. 3 (December 1923): 25–27; "Uncle Ben Dragoo Has Colorful History," *Junction Eagle*, December 22, 1927; "Uncle Ben Dragoo Has Colorful History," *Frontier Times* 5, no. 5 (February 1928): 216–17; and J. Marvin Hunter, "'Uncle' Ben Dragoo, A Texas Ranger," *Frontier Times* 6, no. 7 (April 1929): 287–91.

6. Hunter, "'Uncle' Ben Dragoo, A Texas Ranger," 287.

7. Ibid., 291.

8. Ibid., 290–91.

9. Peter Robertson interview (1920 or 1921), in J. Marvin Hunter, ed., "The Capture of Cynthia Ann Parker," *Frontier Times* 16 (May 1939): 364–65.

10. Ibid.

11. Jonathan Hamilton Baker, Diary of Jonathan Hamilton Baker, manuscript, private collection, Tarrant County Historical Commission, Fort Worth (hereafter cited as Baker, Diary—first, manuscript).

12. Jonathan Hamilton Baker, Diary of Jonathan [James] Hamilton Baker, 1858–1918, typescript, Dolph Briscoe Center for American History, University of Texas at Austin (hereafter cited as Baker, Diary—second, typescript).

13. Baker, Diary—first, manuscript, entry for December 20, 1860.

14. Baker, Diary—second, typescript.

15. Francis M. Peveler, "Reminiscences" (notes to J. Evetts Haley), October 14, 1932, in Nita Stewart Haley Memorial Library and J. Evetts Haley History Center, Midland, Texas. Peveler's account is also in G. A. Holland, *History of Parker County and the Double Log Cabin*, 49–52.

16. Peveler, "Reminiscences."

17. Holland, *History of Parker County*, 50–51.

18. Peveler, "Reminiscences."

19. Ibid.; U.S. Department of War, Returns from U.S. Military Posts, 1800–1916, Camp Cooper, November 1860 to January 1861, Roll 253, Microfilm Copy M-617, RG94, NA (hereafter cited as Post Returns, Camp Cooper).

20. Charles Goodnight, "My Recollections and Memories of the Capture of Cynthia Ann Parker," as told to J. Evetts Haley, Charles Goodnight, Papers, Panhandle-Plains Historical Museum, Canyon, Texas.

21. Ibid. See also J. Evetts Haley, ed, "Charles Goodnight's Indian Recollections," *Panhandle-Plains Historical Review* 1 (1928): 3–29; J. Evetts Haley, *Charles Goodnight: Cowman and Plainsman*, 51–61.

22. Haley, "Charles Goodnight's Indian Recollections," 3–29.

23. Ibid.

24. Ibid.; Rogers, "Recollections"; Baker, Diary—first, manuscript, entry for December 20, 1860.

25. DeShields, *Cynthia Ann Parker*, 42.

26. John W. Spangler, First Sergeant, Company H, to Nathan G. Evans, Captain, Second Cavalry, Camp Cooper, December 24, 1860, NA, photocopy in possession of authors.

27. John W. Spangler to Nathan G. Evans, January 16, 1861, in *San Antonio Ledger*, February 2, 1861, as cited in Selden, *Return*, 292–94.

28. Captain L. S. Ross to Governor Sam Houston, January 4, 1861, as cited in "More about the Capture of Woman Prisoner," *San Antonio Express*, February 23, 1908, and in "Cynthia Ann Parker Again," *Beeville Bee*, February 28, 1908. A copy of the report is also in Eric C. Caren, comp., *Texas Extra: A Newspaper History of the Lone Star State, 1835–1935*, 103.

29. Spangler to Evans, January 16, 1861.

## Chapter 3

1. Gregg Cantrell, "The Bones of Stephen F. Austin: History and Memory in Progressive-Era Texas," in *Lone Star Pasts: Memory and History in Texas*, ed. Gregg Cantrell and Elizabeth Hayes Turner, 50–51.

2. Judith Ann Benner, *Sul Ross: Soldier, Statesman, Educator*, 58.

3. James T. DeShields, *Cynthia Ann Parker*, xiii.

4. Ibid., 44.

5. Ibid., 43.

6. Elizabeth Ross Clark, "Life of Sul Ross," 61, in Ross Family Papers, 1859–1898, 1927–1931, Texas Collection Archives, Baylor University.

7. Lawrence T. Jones III, "Cynthia Ann Parker and Pease Ross—The Forgotten

Photographs," *Southwestern Historical Quarterly* 93, no. 3 (January 1990): 379–84; Benner, *Sul Ross*, 55n29.

8. Marion T. Brown to "home folk," December 13, 1886, in C. Richard King, ed., *Marion T. Brown: Letters from Fort Sill, 1886–1887*, 30.

9. James T. DeShields, *Border Wars of Texas*, 163

10. J. W. Wilbarger, *Indian Depredations in Texas*, 335–39; Robert H. Williams, "The Case for Peta Nocona," *Texana* 10, no. 1 (1972): 55–72.

11. Jonathan Hamilton Baker, Diary of Jonathan Hamilton Baker, December 19, 1860, entry, manuscript, private collection, Tarrant County Historical Commission, Fort Worth (hereafter cited as Baker, Diary—first, manuscript).

12. "From the Frontier," *Dallas Herald*, January 2, 1861.

13. Captain L. S. Ross to Governor Sam Houston, January 4, 1861, as it appeared in "More about the Capture of Woman Prisoner," *San Antonio Express,* February 23, 1908, and in "Cynthia Ann Parker Again," *Beeville Bee*, February 28, 1908. The report is also found in Eric C. Caren, comp., *A Newspaper History of the Lone Star State, 1835–1935*, 103.

14. J. Evetts Haley, *Charles Goodnight: Cowman and Plainsman*, 56n7.

15. "More about the Capture of Woman Prisoner," *San Antonio Express*, February 23, 1908; "Cynthia Ann Parker Again," *Beeville Bee*, February 28, 1908; Francis B. Heitman, *Historical Register and Dictionary of the United States Army*, 1:638.

16. Amelia W. Williams and Eugene C. Barker, eds., *The Writings of Sam Houston, 1813–1863*, 8:240.

17. Ross to Houston, January 4, 1861.

18. "The Parker Captives," *Galveston News*, June 3, 1875; "The Parker Captives," *Dallas Weekly Herald*, June 19, 1875.

19. "The Parker Captives," *Galveston News*, June 3, 1875.

20. Sul Ross to Victor M. Rose, October 5, 1880, in Perry Wayne Shelton, comp., *Personal Civil War Letters of General Lawrence Sullivan Ross with Other Letters*, 79–80.

21. Ross to Rose, April 21, 1881, in ibid., 85.

22. The "a correct history" quote is in "The Parker Captives," *Galveston News*, June 3, 1875. The Peta Nocona statement is in DeShields, *Cynthia Ann Parker*, 41–44.

23. DeShields, *Cynthia Ann Parker*, 42. The "great, greasy lazy buck" quote from Victor M. Rose as told to James DeShields is in ibid., 17, and repeated in Wil-

liams, "The Case for Peta Nocona," 72n26. The Horace Jones quotes are in "Marion's Indian Notes from Interpreter H. P. Jones, Jany. 1887," and Brown to her father, December 20, 1886, in King, *Marion T. Brown*, 78 and 36, respectively.

24. "Padgitt Replies to Quanah Parker," *Dallas Morning News*, November 21, 1909.

25. Ibid.

26. Peter Robertson interview (1920 or 1921), in J. Marvin Hunter, ed., "The Capture of Cynthia Ann Parker," *Frontier Times* 16 (May 1939): 364–65.

27. "The Parker Captives," *Galveston News*, June 3, 1875; "The Parker Captives," *Dallas Weekly Herald*, June 19, 1875; DeShields, *Cynthia Ann Parker*, 41–44; Wilbarger, *Indian Depredations in Texas*, 335–39; Benjamin F. Gholson interview with Felix Williams and Harvey Chelsey, August 26, 1931, in Rupert N. Richardson, ed., "The Death of Nocona and the Recovery of Cynthia Ann Parker," *Southwestern Historical Quarterly* 46 (July 1942): 15–42 (hereafter cited as Gholson interview, 1931); and Benjamin F. Gholson, "Recollections of B. F. Gholson," as told to J. A. Rickard, August 1928, typescript, Dolph Briscoe Center for American History, University of Texas at Austin (hereafter cited as Gholson, "Recollections," 1928).

28. Baker, Diary—first, manuscript, entry for December 19, 1860.

29. Ibid., entry for December 21, 1860.

30. "Padgitt Replies to Quanah Parker," *Dallas Morning News*, November 21, 1909.

31. Robertson interview, in Hunter, "The Capture of Cynthia Ann Parker," 364–65.

32. "Ben Dragoo Tells of the Capture of Cynthia Ann Parker," *Frontier Times* 1, no. 3 (December 1923): 25–27. See also J. Marvin Hunter, "'Uncle' Ben Dragoo, a Texas Ranger," *Frontier Times* 6, no. 7 (April 1929): 287–91.

33. "Indian News," *Galveston Civilian and Gazette*, January 15, 1861.

34. Ross to Houston, January 4, 1861.

35. Gholson interview, 1931, 15–21; Gholson, "Recollections," 1928, 3–29.

36. Ross to Rose, June 1, 1878, in Shelton, *Personal Civil War Letters of General Lawrence Sullivan Ross*, 74.

37. Susan Parker St. John, cousin of Cynthia Ann, interview with L. S. Ross, President, Texas A&M College, 1894, Joseph Taulman Papers, Dolph Briscoe Center for American History, University of Texas at Austin.

38. John W. Spangler, First Sergeant, Company H, to Nathan G. Evans, Captain, Second Cavalry, Camp Cooper, December 24, 1860, NA, photocopy in possession of authors.

39. John W. Spangler to Nathan Evans, January 16, 1861, in *San Antonio Ledger*, February 2, 1861, as cited in Selden, *Return*, 292–94.

40. J. Frank Dobie, *Cow People*, 287–88.

## Chapter 4

1. See, for example, Jo Ella Powell Exley, *Frontier Blood: The Saga of the Parker Family*; Judith Ann Benner, *Sul Ross: Soldier, Statesman, Educator*; Charles M. Robinson III, *The Men Who Wear the Star: The Story of the Texas Rangers*; and Robert H. Williams, "The Case for Peta Nocona," *Texana* 10, no. 1 (1972): 55–72.

2. Benjamin F. Gholson interview with Felix Williams and Harvey Chelsey, August 26, 1931, in Rupert N. Richardson, ed., "The Death of Nocona and the Recovery of Cynthia Ann Parker," *Southwestern Historical Quarterly* 46 (July 1942): 15–21 (hereafter cited as Gholson interview, 1931); Benjamin F. Gholson, "Recollections of B. F. Gholson," as told to J. A. Rickard, August 1928, typescript, Dolph Briscoe Center for American History, University of Texas at Austin (hereafter cited as Gholson, "Recollections," 1928).

3. Gholson, "Recollections," 1928, 6, 23. See also Donna Gholson Cook, *Gholson Road: Revolutionaries and Texas Rangers*, 262.

4. Ibid.

5. Jonathan Hamilton Baker, Diary of Jonathan Hamilton Baker, manuscript, December 19, 1860, entry, private collection, Tarrant County Historical Commission, Fort Worth (hereafter cited as Baker, Diary—first, manuscript).

6. "From the Frontier," *Dallas Herald*, January 2, 1861.

7. Sul Ross to Governor Sam Houston, January 4, 1861, as cited in "More about the Capture of Woman Prisoner," *San Antonio Express*, February 23, 1908, and in "Cynthia Ann Parker Again," *Beeville Bee*, February 28, 1908. A copy of the report is also in Eric C. Caren, comp., *Texas Extra: A Newspaper History of the Lone Star State, 1835–1935*, 103.

8. John W. Spangler, First Sergeant, Company H, to Nathan G. Evans, Captain, Second Cavalry, Camp Cooper, December 24, 1860, National Archives, photocopy in possession of authors.

NOTES

9. Baker, Diary—first, manuscript. See also Jonathan Hamilton Baker, Diary of Jonathan [James] Hamilton Baker, 1858–1918, typescript, Dolph Briscoe Center for American History, University of Texas at Austin (hereafter cited as Baker, Diary—second, typescript).

10. Gholson, "Recollections," 1928, 3–29; Gholson interview, 1931, 16; "From the Frontier," *Dallas Herald*, January 2, 1861; Ross to Houston, January 4, 1861; Baker, Diary—first, manuscript.

11. "Ben Dragoo Tells of the Capture of Cynthia Ann Parker," *Frontier Times* 1, no. 3 (December 1923): 25–27. The other error was the identity of the person who captured Cynthia Ann Parker.

12. Spangler to Evans, December 24, 1860; John W. Spangler to Nathan Evans, January 16, 1861, in *San Antonio Ledger*, February 2, 1861, as cited in Jack K. Selden, *Return: The Parker Story*, 292–94; Ross to Houston, January 4, 1861; Gholson interview, 1931, 16–20; James T. DeShields, *Cynthia Ann Parker*, 44–45. The Spangler report of December 24, 1860, apparently substitutes Lt. "Callahan" for Kelliher, as there was no "Callahan" among Ross's troops.

13. "Ben Dragoo Tells of the Capture of Cynthia Ann Parker," *Frontier Times* 1, no. 3 (December 1923): 25–27. See also "Uncle Ben Dragoo Has Colorful History," *Frontier Times* 5, no. 5 (February 1928): 216–17; and J. Marvin Hunter, "'Uncle' Ben Dragoo, A Texas Ranger, *Frontier Times* 6, no. 7 (April 1929): 287–91.

14. Peter Robertson interview (1920 or 1921), in J. Marvin Hunter, ed., "The Capture of Cynthia Ann Parker," *Frontier Times* 16 (May 1939): 364–65.

15. Harvey Chelsey quoted in Walter Prescott Webb, "Texas Collection," *Southwestern Historical Quarterly* 46 (July 1942): 63.

16. Muster Roll/Payroll, John Williams Company, Texas Rangers, no. 117, Records, Clem R. Johns, Comptroller of State of Texas, Texas State Archives, Austin. See also Robert W. Stephens, *Texas Rangers Indian War Pensions*, vi.

17. Declaration for Survivor's Pension—Indian Wars, United States Pension Office, for B. F. Gholson, April 16, 1917, Lampasas County, photocopy, Texas State Archives, Austin (hereafter cited as Gholson Pension Application).

18. Ibid.

19. Muster Roll/Payroll, L. S. Ross Company, Texas Rangers, November 17, 1860, in Records, C. R. Johns, Comptroller of the State of Texas, Texas State Archives, Austin.

20. Gholson Pension Application.

21. Adjutant General, State of Texas, to Commissioner of Pensions, Washington, D.C., July 1, 1919, and Department of the Interior, Bureau of Pensions, July 27, 1927, both in Texas State Archives, Austin. See also Judith Ann Benner, *Sul Ross: Soldier, Statesman, Educator*, 40.

## Chapter 5

1. Elaine Pagels, *The Gnostic Gospels*, 151; Will Bagley, *Blood of the Prophets: Brigham Young and the Massacre at Mountain Meadows*, 335.

2. The Comanche perspective is found in Paul I. Wellman, "Cynthia Ann Parker," *Chronicles of Oklahoma* 12, no. 2 (1934): 163–70. But see also "Marion's Indian Notes from the Interpreter H. P. Jones, Jany. 1887," in C. Richard King, ed., *Marion T. Brown: Letters from Fort Sill, 1886–1887*, 77–79; Brown to her mother, December 26, 1886, in ibid., 38. Sul Ross himself says he killed Mohee in "The Parker Captives," *Galveston News*, June 3, 1875, and the *Dallas Weekly Herald*, June 19, 1875.

3. James T. DeShields, *Cynthia Ann Parker*, 42.

4. "Padgitt Replies to Quanah Parker," *Dallas Morning News*, November 21, 1909. See also "The Killing of Chief Peta Nocona," *Frontier Times* 4, no. 3 (December 1926): 42–43.

5. Robert H. Williams, "The Case for Peta Nocona," *Texana* 10, no. 1 (1972): 55–72.

6. Robert M. Utley, *Lone Star Justice: The First Century of the Texas Rangers*, 324n36.

7. Benjamin F. Gholson interview with Felix Williams and Harvey Chelsey, August 26, 1931, in Rupert N. Richardson, ed., "The Death of Nocona and the Recovery of Cynthia Ann Parker," *Southwestern Historical Quarterly* 46 (July 1942): 15–42 (hereafter cited as Gholson interview, 1931). See also Benjamin F. Gholson, "Recollections of B. F. Gholson," as told to J. A. Rickard, August 1928, typescript, the Dolph Briscoe Center for American History, University of Texas at Austin (hereafter cited as Gholson, "Recollections," 1928).

8. Williams, "The Case for Peta Nocona," 71n4; Gholson interview, 1931, 68.

9. Harvey Chelsey quoted in Walter Prescott Webb, "Texas Collection," *Southwestern Historical Quarterly* 46 (July 1942): 63. Harvey Chelsey's name is also spelled Hervey Chesley, as in Richardson, "Death of Nocona," n7.

10. Gholson interview, 1931, 16–17.

11. Williams, "The Case for Peta Nocona," 55.

12. Ibid.

13. Ibid., 56.

14. Ibid.

15. "Quanah Parker Sets History Straight," *Semi-Weekly Farm News* (Dallas), October 29, 1909; "Padgitt Replies to Quanah Parker," *Dallas Morning News*, November 11, 1909.

16. Marion T. Brown to her mother, January 27, 1887, in King, *Marion T. Brown*, 63. See also Brown to her father, December 20, 1886, in ibid., 35; J. Evetts Haley, ed., "Charles Goodnight's Indian Recollections," *Panhandle-Plains Historical Review* 1 (1928): 3–29; and Williams, "The Case for Peta Nocona," 56, 62.

17. Williams, "The Case for Peta Nocona," 55–58.

18. Ibid., 58–59.

19. Gholson interview, 1931, 18–19.

20. Haley, "Charles Goodnight's Indian Recollections," 25; Williams, "The Case for Peta Nocona," 59.

21. "The Parker Captives," *Galveston News*, June 3, 1875; "The Parker Captives," *Dallas Weekly Herald*, June 19, 1875; DeShields, *Cynthia Ann Parker*, 43–44.

22. Williams, "The Case for Peta Nocona," 59.

23. Elizabeth Ross Clark, "Life of Sul Ross," 61, in Ross Family Papers, 1859–1989, 1927–1931, Texas Collection, Archives, Baylor University.

24. Stephen E. Ambrose, *The Victors, Eisenhower and His Boys: The Men of World War II* (New York: Simon & Schuster, 1998).

25. "The Parker Captives," *Galveston News*, June 3, 1875; "The Parker Captives," *Dallas Weekly Herald*, June 19, 1875.

26. "The Parker Captives," *Galveston News*, June 3, 1875; "The Parker Captives," *Dallas Weekly Herald*, June 19, 1875; and John Henry Brown's response in "'The Parker Captives'—General L. S. Ross," *Dallas Weekly Herald*, June 19, 1875.

27. Nathan G. Evans, Captain, Second Cavalry, Camp Cooper, to Maj. W. A. Nichols, Department of Texas, San Antonio, December 26, 1860, Records Relating to Military Posts, Camp Cooper, Letters Sent, RG393, NA.

28. Williams, "The Case for Peta Nocona," 63. The Goodnight quote is on pp. 62–63.

29. Williams, "The Case for Peta Nocona," 63. See also J. Evetts Haley, *Charles Goodnight: Cowman and Plainsman*, 57, and Haley, "Charles Goodnight's Indian Recollections, 25.

30. Williams, "The Case for Peta Nocona," 63.

31. Gholson, "Recollections," 1928, 3–23.

32. Hiram B. Rogers, "Recollections of Ranger H. B. Rogers of the Capture of Cynthia Ann Parker," as told to J. A. Rickard, n.d., filed with Benjamin Franklin Gholson, "Recollections of B. F. Gholson," as told to J. A. Rickard, August 1928, in the Dolph Briscoe Center for American History, University of Texas at Austin; Peter Robertson interview (1920 or 1921), in J. Marvin Hunter, ed., "The Capture of Cynthia Ann Parker," *Frontier Times* 16 (May 1939): 364–65.

33. Williams, "The Case for Peta Nocona," 69.

34. Ibid., 66.

35. "The Parker Captives," *Dallas Weekly Herald*, June 19, 1875; "'The Parker Captives'—General L. S. Ross," *Dallas Weekly Herald*, June 19, 1875; John Henry Brown, *Indian Wars and Pioneers of Texas*, 42.

36. Williams, "The Case for Peta Nocona," 56–58.

37. Ibid., 71n7.

38. Ibid., 65–66. For a Comanche explanation of such reticence, see Paul I. Wellman, "Cynthia Ann Parker," *Chronicles of Oklahoma* 12, no. 2 (June 1934): 165.

39. Brown to her father, John Henry Brown, December 20, 1886, in King, *Letters from Fort Sill*, 35.

40. "Marion's Indian Notes from Interpreter H. P. Jones, Jany. 1887," in ibid., 77–79.

41. "Quanah Route Day Draws Large Crowd" and "Straightens Out History," *Dallas Morning News*, October 25, 1910.

42. "Straightens Out History," *Dallas Morning News*, October 25, 1910.

43. "Quanah Parker Sets History Straight," *Semi-Weekly Farm News* (Dallas), October 29, 1909. See also *Dallas Morning News*, October 27, 1909; *Dallas Daily Times Herald*, October 27, 1909.

44. "Quanah Route Day," *Dallas Daily Times Herald*, October 26, 1909.

45. "An Historical Error Corrected," *Indian Craftsman*, 2, no. 5 (January 1910): 28.

46. Gholson, "Recollections," 1928, 3–23.

47. Evans to Nichols, December 26, 1860.

# NOTES

48. U.S. Department of War, Returns from United States Military Posts, 1800–1916, Camp Cooper, November 1860 to January 1861, Roll 253, Microfilm Copy M-617, RG94, NA; H. E. Alvord to E. J. Davis, Governor of Texas, September 22, 1873, in Dorman H. Winfrey and James M. Day, eds., *The Indian Papers of Texas and the Southwest, 1825–1916*, 4:348–49; Peter Cozzens, ed., *Eyewitnesses to the Indian Wars, 1865–1890*, 5:282.

49. Thomas Gladwin, "Comanche Kin Behavior," *American Anthropologist* 50 (January–March 1948): 75; Lila Wistrand-Robinson and James Armagost, *Comanche Dictionary and Grammar*, 31, 90, 184, 201.

50. Gladwin, "Comanche Kin Behavior," 79, 82, and 83–94. See also W. W. Newcomb, Jr., *The Indians of Texas: From Prehistoric to Modern Times*, 170; and Stanley Noyes, *Los Comanches: The Horse People, 1751–1845*, 196. See also Pekka Hämäläinen, *The Comanche Empire*, 248–50.

51. Gregory R. Campbell, *An Ethnological and Ethnohistorical Assessment of Ethnobotanical and Cultural Resources of Bent's Old Fort National Historic Site and the Sand Creek National Historic Site*, 611; Gladwin, "Comanche Kin Behavior," 74–75; Wistrand-Robinson and Armagost, *Comanche Dictionary and Grammar*, 91, 184, 189, 194, 219, 227; and Noyes, *Los Comanches*, 27.

52. Williams, "The Case for Peta Nocona," 54–56; Campbell, *An Ethnological and Ethnohistorical Assessment*, 611. See also Gerald Betty, *Comanche Society before the Reservation*, 43; and Ernest Wallace and E. Adamson Hoebel, *The Comanches: Lords of the South Plains*, 125–27.

53. "Quanah Parker," *The Arrow* (publication of the Carlisle Indian Industrial School, Carlisle, Pa.), March 9, 1905.

54. Williams, "The Case for Peta Nocona," 71n2; Quanah Parker to Charles Goodnight, ca. 1911, in Charles Goodnight Papers, Panhandle-Plains Historical Museum. Williams includes the letter in "The Case for Peta Nocona," 56–58. See also Hämäläinen, *Comanche Empire*, 247–51.

55. Gholson, "Recollections," 1928; Parker to Goodnight, ca. 1911, and as cited in Williams, "The Case for Peta Nocona," 57.

56. Gladwin, "Comanche Kin Behavior," 86. See also Wallace and Hoebel, *The Comanches*, 141, 144–45; Hämäläinen, *Comanche Empire*, 247–51; Noyes, *Los Comanches*, 94; and Newcomb, *Indians of Texas*, 170–71.

57. Brown, letter to her mother, January 27, 1887, in King, *Letters from Fort Sill*, 65.

# NOTES

## Chapter 6

1. James DeShields, *Cynthia Ann Parker*, 58–68.

2. "The Parker Captives—General L. S. Ross," *Dallas Weekly Herald*, June 19, 1875.

3. John Henry Brown, *Indian Wars and Pioneers of Texas*, 317.

4. Marion T. Brown to her "home folk," December 13, 1886, in C. Richard King, ed., *Marion T. Brown: Letters From Fort Sill, 1886–1887*, 30.

5. Brown to her father, December 19, 1886, in ibid., 33.

6. Brown to her father, December 20, 1886, 34–36, and "Marion's Indian Notes from Interpreter H. P. Jones, Jany. 1887," 78, both in ibid.

7. Brown to her father, December 20, 1886, in ibid., 35.

8. Brown to her mother, January 27, 1887, in ibid., 65.

9. Brown to her father, December 20, 1886, in ibid., 36.

10. Williams, "The Case for Peta Nocona," 57.

11. Brown, *Indian Wars and Pioneers of Texas*, 42, 317.

12. John H. Jenkins, *Basic Texas Books*, 59.

13. J. Marvin Hunter, "The Capture of Cynthia Ann Parker," *Frontier Times* 16, no. 8 (May 1939): 365.

14. J. Marvin Hunter, "'Uncle' Ben Dragoo, a Texas Ranger," *Frontier Times* 6, no. 7 (April 1929): 291.

15. See, for example, Marion T. Brown's letters, particularly January 27, 1887, in King, *Marion T. Brown*, 63.

16. Will Bagley, *Blood of the Prophets: Brigham Young and the Massacre at Mountain Meadows*, xvi.

17. See, for example, Judith Ann Benner, *Sul Ross: Soldier, Statesman, Educator*; Jo Ella Powell Exley, *Frontier Blood: The Saga of the Parker Family*; Doyle Marshall, *A Cry Unheard: The Story of Indian Attacks in and around Parker County, Texas, 1858–1872*; J. Evetts Haley, *Charles Goodnight: Cowman and Plainsman*; and Joseph Carroll McConnell, *The West Texas Frontier*.

18. See, for example, McConnell, *West Texas Frontier*; James R. Arnold, *Jeff Davis's Own: Cavalry, Comanches, and the Battle for the Texas Frontier*; Benner, *Sul Ross*; Exley, *Frontier Blood*; Charles M. Robinson III, *The Men Who Wear the Star: The Story of the Texas Rangers*; Frederick Wilkins, *Defending Borders: The Texas Rangers, 1848–1861*; and Robert H. Williams, "The Case for Peta Nocona."

19. Margaret Schmidt Hacker, *Cynthia Ann Parker: The Life and the Legend*, 21.

20. The Quanah biographies include Bill Neeley, *Quanah Parker and His People*, which is a fictionalized account, and *The Last Comanche Chief: The Life and Times of Quanah Parker*, Charles H. Sommer, *Quanah Parker: Last Chief of the Comanches*; and Zoe A. Tilghman, *Quanah, The Eagle of the Comanches*, another fictionalized biography.

21. William T. Hagan, *Quanah Parker, Comanche Chief*, 6–7.

22. See, for example, Benner, *Sul Ross*.

23. Robert M. Utley, *Lone Star Justice: The First Century of the Texas Rangers*; Mike Cox, *The Texas Rangers*.

24. See, for example, Robinson, *The Men Who Wear the Star*; Roger N. Conger et al., *Rangers of Texas*; and Albert Bigelow Paine, *Captain Bill McDonald, Texas Ranger: A Story of Frontier Reform*.

25. Gary Clayton Anderson, *The Conquest of Texas: Ethnic Cleansing in the Promised Land, 1829–1875*, 331–32, 451n25. For a contrary opinion, see Gerald Betty, *Comanche Society before the Reservation*, 4.

26. Carl Coke Rister, *Robert E. Lee in Texas*, 147–48.

27. Odie B. Faulk, *Crimson Desert: Indian Wars of the American Southwest*, 107, 208.

28. Rupert Norval Richardson, *The Frontier of Northwest Texas, 1846–1876*, 210–11.

29. Ida Lasater Huckabay, *Ninety-four Years in Jack County, 1854–1948*, 66–68.

30. Thomas W. Kavanagh, *Comanche Political History: An Ethnohistorical Perspective, 1706–1875*, 373.

31. Betty, *Comanche Society before the Reservation*, 4

32. Rupert Norval Richardson, *Comanche Barrier to South Plains Settlement*, 40, 134.

33. Stanley Noyes, *Los Comanches: The Horse People, 1751–1845*, 307–308. See also Ninth Census of the United States, 1870, Roll M 593, p. 212, Schedule 1—Inhabitants in Anderson County, Texas, Post Office: Palestine, RG29, NA; and Jack K. Selden, *Return: The Parker Story*, 208n***.

34. T. R. Fehrenbach, *Comanches: The Destruction of a People*, 439–41.

35. Paul I. Wellman, "Cynthia Ann Parker," *Chronicles of Oklahoma* 12, no. 2 (June 1934): 165–66.

36. Ibid., 168–69.

37. Ibid., 167–69.

# NOTES

38. J. W. (Bud) Ellison, "Scouted on Pease River," *Frontier Times* 5, no. 3 (December 1927): 100–101.

39. Randolph B. Campbell, *Gone to Texas: A History of the Lone Star State*, 205–206.

40. T. R. Fehrenbach, *Lone Star: A History of Texas and the Texans*, 544–45.

41. Ernest Wallace, *Texas in Turmoil*, 26–27.

42. Seymour V. Connor, *Texas: A History*, 169.

43. Henry David Thoreau, *Walden; or, Life in the Woods*, 204.

# APPENDIX
## A Chronology of Participant and Eyewitness Accounts

1. December 19, 1860. **Jonathan H. Baker**, in his diary entry for this date, reported that **Captain Lawrence S. "Sul" Ross** told Captain J. J. "Jack" Cureton's militia company, shortly after the fight along Mule Creek, that the Texas Rangers and federal troops had engaged a party of fifteen Indians. This informal statement was Ross's first account of the half battle, half massacre.

   Baker, one of Cureton's militiamen who did not participate in the incident, was a schoolteacher who wrote daily in his diary. There are two versions of the diary: the original handwritten document in Fort Worth and the later altered and typed copy on file in the Dolph Briscoe Center for American History, the University of Texas at Austin.

2. December 20, 1860. **Jonathan Baker** continued his discussion of events at and near the battlefield. On this day he describes some of the militiamen's actions on the day after the battle.

3. December 23, 1860. **Sul Ross** near Fort Belknap on the return home told a correspondent of the *Dallas Herald* about the battle near the Pease River. The brief account was published in the January 2, 1861, edition of the *Herald*.

4. December 24, 1860. **Sergeant John Spangler**, head of the twenty troops of the U.S. Second Cavalry, sent his report of the Pease River incident to his

superior officer, Captain Nathan Evans, at Camp Cooper in Throckmorton County. Handwritten, it covered two short pages and is located in the military records of the National Archives.

5. January 4, 1861. **Captain Sul Ross** sent his official report to Governor Sam Houston. The report was in the files of the Texas Adjutant General's Office until at least February 1908, and that month it was printed in both the *San Antonio Ledger* and *Beeville Bee*. It is no longer in the files of the Adjutant General's Office, or at least it cannot be found there.

6. January 16, 1861. **Sergeant John Spangler**, at the request of Major W. A. Nichols at the Department of Texas headquarters, issued a second and longer report. It was printed in the *San Antonio Ledger* on February 2, 1861, but the original cannot be found in the military records of the National Archives.

7. June 3 and June 19, 1875. A letter **Sul Ross** had written about three years earlier to the *Galveston News* was finally published and two weeks later published again in the *Dallas Weekly Herald*. The letter represents Ross's fourth account of the Battle of Pease River.

8. 1884 (?). Ross told his story of the Pease River/Mule Creek incident to **James T. DeShields**, a bookseller and friend of Ross. DeShields was writing a book, *Cynthia Ann Parker*, and included in it Ross's fifth or authorized account of the battle.

9. 1894. **Susan Parker St. John**, a first cousin of Cynthia Ann Parker, interviewed Sul Ross in his office at the Agricultural and Mechanical College of Texas (Texas A&M). St. John's notes are in the Joseph Taulman Papers at the Dolph Briscoe Center for American History, the University of Texas at Austin.

10. November 21, 1909. **Tom Padgitt**, Sul Ross's brother-in-law, published a letter in the *Dallas Morning News* that contained information about the battle Ross had told him over the years.

11. 1920 or 1921. **Peter Robertson**, a scout for the militiamen, gave his account of the Pease River incident. Editors of *Frontier Times* published the statement in the May 1939 issue of their journal.

12. December 1923. **Benjamin C. Dragoo**, a Texas Ranger, published his story of the Pease River battle in *Frontier Times*. A different Dragoo story was printed in the *Junction Eagle* in December 1927 and a portion of it reprinted in the February 1928 edition of *Frontier Times*. Then in April 1929 the larger story, which included the 1923 version, again appeared in *Frontier Times*.

13. November 13, 1926. **Charles Goodnight**, a scout for the militiamen, told his story of the Pease River battle to J. Evetts Haley, Goodnight's biographer. Goodnight's account, edited by J. Evetts Haley, appears in *Charles Goodnight's Indian Recollections* (1926), the first edition of the *Panhandle Plains Historical Review* (1928), and Haley's biography of the Texas Panhandle rancher, *Charles Goodnight: Cowman and Plainsman* (1935).

14. 1928. **Hiram B. Rogers**, a Texas Ranger, gave his brief account to J. A. Rickard, who included it with the 1928 reminiscences of Benjamin F. Gholson that are located in the Dolph Briscoe Center for American History, the University of Texas at Austin.

15. August 1928. **Benjamin Franklin Gholson** gave an account of the Pease River incident to J. A. Rickard, but Gholson was not at the Mule Creek fight. The interview is in the Dolph Briscoe Center for American History at the University of Texas at Austin.

16. August 1931. **Benjamin Gholson** gave a second account of the 1860 battle, this one to Felix Williams and Harvey Chelsey. The 1931 reminiscences were published in the *Southwestern Historical Quarterly* for July 1942.

17. October 14, 1932. **Francis M. Peveler**, a member of Jack Cureton's militiamen, wrote a letter to J. Evetts Haley. The letter is on file in the Nita Stewart Haley Memorial Library and J. Evetts Haley History Center in Midland, Texas.

# BIBLIOGRAPHY

## Manuscript Sources

Adjutant General, State of Texas. Letter to Commissioner of Pensions, Washington, D.C., July 1, 1919. Photocopy. Texas State Archives, Austin.

Baker, Jonathan Hamilton. Diary of Jonathan Hamilton Baker. Manuscript. Private collection, Tarrant County Historical Commission, Fort Worth.

———. Diary of Jonathan [James] Hamilton Baker, 1858–1918. Typescript. Dolph Briscoe Center for American History, University of Texas at Austin.

Dillard, Raymond L. "A History of the Ross Family and Its Most Distinguished Member, Lawrence Sullivan Ross." M.A. thesis, Baylor University, 1931.

Gholson, Benjamin F. Interview with Felix Williams and Harvey Chelsey, August 26, 1931. Typescript. Filed with Walter Prescott Webb Papers, Dolph Briscoe Center for American History, University of Texas at Austin.

———. "Reminiscences of B. F. Gholson," as told to J. A. Rickard, August 1928. Typescript. Dolph Briscoe Center for American History, University of Texas at Austin.

———. "Record of Service—Indian Wars," July 1, 1919. Texas Adjutant General's Department, Austin.

Goodnight, Charles. Papers. Panhandle-Plains Historical Museum, Canyon, Texas.

Peveler, Francis M. "Reminiscences" (notes to J. Evetts Haley), October 14, 1932.

Nita Stewart Haley Memorial Library and J. Evetts Haley History Center, Midland, Texas.

Rogers, Hiram B. "Recollections of Ranger H. B. Rogers of the Capture of Cynthia Ann Parker," as told to J. A. Rickard, n.d. Typescript. Filed with Benjamin F. Gholson, "Recollections of B. F. Gholson," as told to J. A. Rickard, August 1928, Dolph Briscoe Center for American History, University of Texas at Austin.

Ross Family Papers, 1859–98, 1927–31. Texas Collection, Archives, Baylor University, Waco, Texas.

Saegert, Laura K., Archivist, Archives Division, Texas State Library, letter to Judge Tom Crum, Hood County, July 1, 1994. Letter in possession of Tom Crum, Granbury, Texas.

Spangler, John W. Report to Nathan G. Evans, Captain, Second Cavalry, Camp Cooper, December 24, 1860. Photocopy in possession of authors.

Taulman, Joseph. Papers. Dolph Briscoe Center for American History, University of Texas at Austin.

Texas Governors. Papers. Archives Division, Texas State Library, Austin.

Texas Rangers, Muster Roll/Payroll Records. L. S. Ross Company, Texas Rangers, November 17, 1860. C. R. Johns, Comptroller of the State of Texas, Texas State Archives, Austin.

U.S., Department of the Interior, Bureau of the Census. Ninth Census of the United States, 1870, Anderson County, Texas, Roll M593, Record Group 29, National Archives and Records Administration, Washington, D.C.

U.S., Department of War. Returns from United States Military Posts, 1800–1916. Camp Cooper, December 1860, Roll 253, Microfilm Copy M-617, Record Group 94, National Archives and Records Administration, Washington, D.C.

———. Records Relating to Military Posts, Camp Cooper, Letters Sent, Record Group 393, National Archives and Records Administration, Washington, D.C.

———. Pension Office. Declaration for Survivor's Pension—Indian Wars, B. F. Gholson, April 16, 1917, Lampasas County. Photocopy. Texas State Archives, Austin.

Vandale, Earl. Collection. Dolph Briscoe Center for American History, University of Texas at Austin.

Webb, Walter Prescott. Papers. Dolph Briscoe Center for American History, University of Texas at Austin.

# BIBLIOGRAPHY

## Newspapers

*Beeville Bee*, 1908.

*Carlton Citizen*, 1938.

*Clarksville Standard*, 1858, 1860.

*Daily Livestock Journal* (Fort Worth), 1909.

*Dallas Daily Times-Herald*, 1909.

*Dallas Herald*, 1861.

*Dallas Morning News*, 1909–10.

*Dallas News*, 1928.

*Dallas Times Herald*, 1910.

*Dallas Weekly Herald*, 1875.

*Galveston Civilian and Gazette*, 1861.

*Galveston News*, 1875.

*Hamilton County News*, 1938.

*Indian Craftsman*, 1910.

*Morning Star* (Carlisle Indian School), 1885.

*The Red Man*, 1910–11.

*San Antonio Ledger*, 1861.

*San Antonio Express*, 1908.

*Semi-Weekly Farm News* (Dallas), 1909.

*Southwestern Farmer and Breeder* (Forth Worth), 1909.

*Wichita Falls Times*, 1910.

## Books and Government Documents

Anderson, Gary Clayton. *The Conquest of Texas: Ethnic Cleansing in the Promised Land, 1820–1875*. Norman: University of Oklahoma Press, 2005.

Arnold, James R. *Jeff Davis's Own: Cavalry, Comanches, and the Battle for the Texas Frontier*. Edison, N.J.: Castle Books, 2007.

Bedford, Hilory G. *Texas Indian Troubles: The Most Thrilling Events in the History of Texas*. Benjamin, Texas: Hargreaves, 1905.

Bagley, Will. *Blood of the Prophets: Brigham Young and the Massacre at Mountain Meadows*. Norman: University of Oklahoma Press, 2004.

Benner, Judith Ann. *Sul Ross: Soldier, Statesman, Educator*. College Station: Texas A&M University Press, 1983.

# BIBLIOGRAPHY

Betty, Gerald. *Comanche Society before the Reservation*. College Station: Texas A&M University Press, 2002.

Bronner, Simon J., ed. *Folk Nation: Folklore in the Creation of American Tradition*. Wilmington, Del.: Scholarly Resources, 2002.

Brown, John Henry. *Indian Wars and Pioneers of Texas*. Austin: L. E. Daniell, 1896; facsimile reprint, Austin: State House Press, 1988.

Buenger, Walter L., and Robert A. Calvert, eds. *Texas Through Time: Evolving Interpretations*. College Station: Texas A&M University Press, 1991.

Campbell, Gregory R. *An Ethnological and Ethnohistorical Assessment of Ethnobotanical and Cultural Resources of Bent's Old Fort National Historic Site and the Sand Creek National Historic Site*, Vols. 1 and 2. Eads, Colo.: National Park Service, Sand Creek National Historic Site, 2007.

Campbell, Randolph B. *Gone to Texas: A History of the Lone Star State*. New York: Oxford University Press, 2003.

Cantrell, Gregg, and Elizabeth Hayes Turner, eds. *Lone Star Pasts: Memory and History in Texas*. Foreword by W. Fitzhugh Brundage. College Station: Texas A&M University Press, 2007.

Caren, Eric C., comp. *Texas Extra: A Newspaper History of the Lone Star State, 1835–1935*. Edison, N.J.: Castle Books, 1999.

Cashion, Ty. *A Texas Frontier: The Clear Fork Country and Fort Griffin, 1849–1887*. Norman: University of Oklahoma Press, 1996.

Chalfant, William Y. *Without Quarter: The Wichita Expedition and the Fight on Crooked Creek*. Foreword by Paul Andrew Hutton. Norman: University of Oklahoma Press, 1991.

Conger, Roger N., et al. *Rangers of Texas*. Introduction by Rupert N. Richardson. Waco: Texian Press, 1969.

Connor, Seymour V. *Texas: A History*. Arlington Heights, Ill.: AHM Publishing Corp., 1971.

Cook, Donna Gholson. *Gholson Road: Revolutionaries and Texas Rangers*. Bloomington, Ind.: 1st Books, 2004.

Cox, Mike. *The Texas Rangers*. 2 vols. New York: Tom Doherty Associates Books, 2008.

Cozzens, Peter, ed. *Eyewitnesses to the Indian Wars, 1865–1890*. 5 vols. Mechanicsburg, Pa.: Stackpole, 2001–2005.

de la Teja, Jesus F., Paula Marks, and Ron Tyler. *Texas, Crossroads of North America: A History.* Boston: Houghton Mifflin, 2004

DeShields, James T. *Border Wars of Texas.* Tioga, Texas: Herald, 1912.

———. *Cynthia Ann Parker.* Saint Louis: n.p., 1886; reprint, with foreword by John Graves, Dallas: Chama Press, 1991.

Dobie, J. Frank, Mody C. Boatright, and Harry H. Ransom, eds. *In the Shadow of History.* Publications of the Texas Folklore Society No. XV. Dallas: Southern Methodist University Press, 1939.

Elkins, John M. *Indian Fighting on the Texas Frontier.* Amarillo: Russell and Cockrell, 1929.

Exley, Jo Ella Powell. *Frontier Blood: The Saga of the Parker Family.* College Station: Texas A&M University Press, 2001.

Faragher, John Mack, ed. *Reading Frederick Jackson Turner.* New York: Henry Holt and Company, 1994.

Faulk, Odie B. *Crimson Desert: Indian Wars of the American Southwest.* New York: Oxford University Press, 1974.

Fehrenbach, T. R. *Comanches: Destruction of a People.* New York: Alfred A. Knopf, 1974.

———. *Lone Star: A History of Texas and Texans.* New York: The Macmillan Company, 1968.

Ford, John S. *Rip Ford's Texas.* Ed. Stephen B. Oates. Austin: University of Texas Press, 1963.

Frantz, Joe B. *Texas: A History.* New York: W. W. Norton & Company, 1976.

Hacker, Margaret Schmidt. *Cynthia Ann Parker: The Life and the Legend.* Southwestern Studies No. 92. El Paso: Texas Western Press, 1990.

Hagan, William T. *Quanah Parker, Comanche Chief.* Norman: University of Oklahoma Press, 1993.

Haley, J. Evetts. *Charles Goodnight: Cowman and Plainsman.* Norman: University of Oklahoma Press, 1935.

———. *Charles Goodnight's Indian Recollections.* Amarillo: Russell and Cockrell, 1926.

Hämäläinen, Pekka. *The Comanche Empire.* New Haven: Yale University Press, 2008.

Hardin, Stephen. *The Texas Rangers.* London: Osprey, 1991.

Heitman, Francis B. *Historical Register and Dictionary of the United States Army*. 2 vols. Washington, D.C.: Government Printing Office, 1903.

*History of the Cattlemen of Texas*. Dallas: The Johnston Printing & Advertising Co., 1914; reprint, Austin: Texas State Historical Association, 1991.

Hoig, Stan. *Tribal Wars of the Southern Plains*. Norman: University of Oklahoma Press, 1993.

Holland, G. A. *History of Parker County and the Double Log Cabin*. Weatherford, Texas: The Herald Publishing Company, 1937.

Holt, Roy D. *Heap Many Texas Chiefs*. San Antonio: The Naylor Company, 1966.

Huckabay, Ida Lasater. *Ninety-four Years in Jack County, 1854–1948*. Waco: Texian Press, 1974.

Hughes, W. J. *Rebellious Ranger: Rip Ford and the Old Southwest*. Foreword by Walter L. Buenger. Norman: University of Oklahoma Press, 1990.

Jackson, Clyde L., and Grace Jackson. *Quanah Parker, Last Chief of the Comanches: A Study in Southwestern Frontier History*. New York: Exposition Press, 1963.

Jackson, Grace. *Cynthia Ann Parker*. San Antonio: The Naylor Company, 1959.

Jenkins, John H. *Basic Texas Books*. Austin: Texas State Historical Association, 1988.

Johnson, Frank W. *A History of Texas and Texans*. 5 vols. Ed. E. C. Barker and E. W. Winkler. Chicago: American Historical Society, 1914 (1916).

Kavanagh, Thomas W., ed. *Comanche Ethnography: Field Notes of E. Adamson Hoebel, Waldo R. Wedel, Gustav G. Carlson, and Robert H. Lowie*. Lincoln: University of Nebraska Press, 2008.

Kavanagh, Thomas W. *Comanche Political History: An Ethnohistorical Perspective, 1706–1875*. Lincoln: University of Nebraska Press, 1996.

Kelton, Elmer, ed. *The Indian in Frontier News*. San Angelo: The Talley Press, 1993.

King, C. Richard, ed. *Marion T. Brown: Letters from Fort Sill, 1886–1887*. Austin: Encino Press, 1970.

La Vere, David. *Life among the Texas Indians: The WPA Narratives*. College Station: Texas A&M University Press, 1998.

———. *The Texas Indians*. College Station: Texas A&M University Press, 2004.

Loftin, Jack. *Trails through Archer*. Austin: Nortex Press, 1979.

Marshall, Doyle. *A Cry Unheard: The Story of Indian Attacks in and around Parker County, Texas, 1858–1872*. Aledo, Texas: Annetta Valley Farm Press, 1990.

Martin, Jack. *Border Boss: Captain John R. Hughes, Texas Ranger*. Austin: State House Press, 1990.

Mayhall, Mildred P. *Indian Wars of Texas*. Waco: Texian Press, 1965.

McComb, David G. *Texas: A Modern History*. Austin: University of Texas Press, 1989.

McConnell, Joseph Carroll. *The West Texas Frontier*. 2 vols. Palo Pinto: Texas Legal Bank & Book Co., 1939.

McDonald, Archie P. *Texas: All Hail the Mighty State*. Austin: Eakin Press, 1983.

Meadows, William C. *Kiowa, Apache, and Comanche Military Societies: Enduring Veterans, 1800 to the Present*. Austin: University of Texas Press, 1999.

Meyer, Carolyn. *Where the Broken Heart Still Beats: The Story of Cynthia Ann Parker*. San Diego, Calif.: Gulliver Books, 1991.

Michno, Gregory F. *Encyclopedia of Indian Wars: Western Battles and Skirmishes, 1850–1890*. Missoula, Mont.: Mountain Press Publishing Company, 2003.

Murrah, David J. *C. C. Slaughter: Rancher, Banker, Baptist*. Austin: University of Texas Press, 1981.

Neeley, Bill. *The Last Comanche Chief: The Life and Times of Quanah Parker*. New York: John Wiley & Sons, 1995.

———. *Quanah Parker and His People*. Slaton, Texas: Brazos Press, 1986.

Neighbours, Kenneth F. *Indian Exodus: Texan Indian Affairs, 1835–1859*. Quanah, Texas: Nortex Press, 1973.

———. *Robert Simpson Neighbors and the Texas Frontier*. Waco: Texian Press, 1975.

Newcomb, W. W., Jr. *The Indians of Texas: From Prehistoric to Modern Times*. Austin: University of Texas Press, 1961.

Noyes, Stanley. *Los Comanches: The Horse People, 1751–1845*. Albuquerque: University of New Mexico Press, 1993.

Nye, W. S. *Carbine and Lance: The Story of Old Fort Sill*. Revised and enlarged. Norman: University of Oklahoma Press, 1969.

O'Connor, Robert F., ed. *Texas Myths*. College Station: Texas A&M University Press, 1986.

Pace, Robert F., and Donald S. Frazier. *Frontier Texas: History of a Borderland to 1880*. Abilene: State House Press, 2004.

Paddock, B. B. *A Twentieth Century History and Biographical Record of North and West Texas*. Chicago: The Lewis Publishing Co., 1906.

Pagels, Elaine. *The Gnostic Gospels.* New York: Random House, 1979.

Paine, Albert Bigelow. *Captain Bill McDonald, Texas Ranger: A Story of Frontier Reform.* Austin: State House Press, 1986.

Ramsey, Jack C. *The Story of Cynthia Ann Parker: Sunshine on the Prairie.* Austin: Eakin Press, 1990.

Richardson, Rupert N., Adrian Anderson, Cary D. Wintz, and Ernest Wallace. *Texas: The Lone Star State.* 9th ed. Upper Saddle River, N.J.: Prentice Hall, 2005.

Richardson, Rupert Norval. *The Comanche Barrier to South Plains Settlement.* Ed. Kenneth R. Jacobs. Austin: Eakin Press, 1996.

———. *The Frontier of Northwest Texas, 1846–1876.* Glendale, Calif.: Arthur H. Clark Co., 1963.

Rister, Carl Coke. *Border Captives.* Norman: University of Oklahoma Press, 1940.

———. *Robert E. Lee in Texas.* Norman: University of Oklahoma Press, 1946.

Robinson, Charles M., III. *The Men Who Wear the Star: The Story of the Texas Rangers.* New York: Random House, 2000.

Roberts, Madge Thornall, ed. *The Personal Correspondence of Sam Houston.* 4 vols. Denton: University of North Texas Press, 2001.

Rupp, Rebecca. *Committed to Memory: How We Remember and Why We Forget.* New York: Crown Publishers, 1998.

Selden, Jack K. *Return: The Parker Story.* Palestine, Texas: Clacton Press, 2006.

Shelton, Perry Wayne. *Personal Civil War Letters of General Lawrence Sullivan Ross with Other Letters.* Austin: Shelly and Richard Morrison, 1994.

Simpson, Harold B. *Cry Comanche: The 2nd U.S. Cavalry in Texas, 1855–1861.* Hillsboro, Texas: Hill College Press, 1988.

Smith, Thomas T. *The Old Army in Texas: A Research Guide to the U.S. Army in Nineteenth-Century Texas.* Austin: Texas State Historical Association, 2000.

Sommer, Charles H. *Quanah Parker: Last Chief of the Comanches.* Saint Louis: Charles H. Sommer, 1945.

Stephens, Robert W. *Texas Rangers Indian War Pensions.* Quanah, Texas: Nortex Press, 1975.

Sterling, William Warren. *Trails and Trials of a Texas Ranger.* Norman: University of Oklahoma Press, 1968.

*The Texas Almanac for 1872.* Galveston: Richardson, Belo & Co., 1872.

Thelen, David, ed. *Memory and American History*. Bloomington: Indiana University Press, 1992.

Thoreau, Henry David. *Walden; or, Life in the Woods*. Mount Vernon, N.Y.: Peter Pauper Press, n.d.

Tilghman, Zoe A. *Quanah, the Eagle of the Comanches*. Oklahoma City: Harlow Publishing Corp., 1938.

Tyler, Ron, et al., eds. *The New Handbook of Texas*. 6 vols. Austin: Texas State Historical Association, 1996.

Uglow, Loyd M. *Standing in the Gap: Army Outposts, Picket Stations, and the Pacification of the Texas Frontier, 1866–1886*. Fort Worth: Texas Christian University Press, n.d.

Untiedt, Kenneth L., ed. *Folklore: In All of Us, In All We Do*. Publications of the Texas Folklore Society LXIII. Denton: University of North Texas Press, 2006.

Utley, Robert M. *Lone Star Justice: The First Century of the Texas Rangers*. New York: Oxford University Press, 2002.

Wallace, Ernest. *Texas in Turmoil*. Austin: Steck-Vaughn Company, 1965.

———, and E. Adamson Hoebel. *The Comanches: Lords of the South Plains*. Norman: University of Oklahoma Press, 1952.

Webb, Walter Prescott. *The Texas Rangers*. New York: Houghton Mifflin Co., 1935.

Whisenhunt, Donald W., ed. *Texas: A Sesquicentennial Celebration*. Austin: Eakin Press, 1984.

Wilbarger, J. W. *Indian Depredations in Texas*. Austin: Hutchings Printing House 1889; facsimile reprint, Austin: The Steck Company, 1935.

Wilkins, Frederick. *Defending Borders: The Texas Rangers, 1848–1861*. Austin: State House Press, 2001.

Williams, Amelia W., and Eugene C. Barker, eds. *The Writings of Sam Houston, 1813–1863*. 8 vols. Austin: University of Texas Press, 1943.

Winfred, Dorman H., and James M. Day, eds. *The Indian Papers of Texas and the Southwest, 1825–1916*. 4 vols., with new introduction by Michael L. Tate. Austin: Texas State Historical Association, 1995.

Wistrand-Robinson, Lila, and James Armagost. *Comanche Dictionary and Grammar*. Publications in Linguistics, No. 92. Arlington: University of Texas at Arlington, 1998.

Wood, Norman B. *Lives of Famous Indian Chiefs*. Chicago: L. W. Walter Company, 1906.

## Articles and Book Chapters

"Ben Dragoo Tells of the Capture of Cynthia Ann Parker." *Frontier Times* 1, no. 3 (December 1923): 25–27.

Boswell, Mack. "Capture of Cynthia Ann Parker." *Frontier Times* 24, no. 12 (September 1947): 532–36.

"Chief Quanah Parker, the Last Great Ruler of the Comanches—Francis E. Leupp in the *Boston Transcript*." *The Red Man* 3, no. 7 (March 1911): 291–96.

Connally, E. L., ed. "Capture of Cynthia Ann Parker." *Texana* 2 (1964): 74–77.

Crimmins, M. L. "Camp Cooper and Fort Griffin, Texas." *West Texas Historical Association Year Book* 17 (1941): 32–43.

———. "First Sergeant John W. Spangler, Company H, Second United States Cavalry." *West Texas Historical Association Year Book* 26 (1950): 68–75.

———. "Major Earl Van Dorn in Texas." *West Texas Historical Association Year Book* 16 (1940): 121–29.

Crum, Tom. "Camp Cooper: A Different Look." *West Texas Historical Association Year Book* 68 (1992): 62–75.

———. "Folklorization of the Battle on Pease River." *West Texas Historical Association Year Book* 72 (1996): 69–85.

———. "Is It Folklore or History? The Answer May Be Important." In Kenneth L. Untiedt, ed. *Folklore: In All of Us, In All We Do*. Publications of the Texas Folklore Society LXIII, 3–11. Denton: University of North Texas Press, 2006.

———. "A Lawyer Looks at Historical Research." *West Texas Historical Association Year Book* 79 (2003): 170–78.

Day, James M., ed. "Two Quanah Parker Letters." *Chronicles of Oklahoma* 44 (Autumn 1966): 313–18.

Donnell, B. D. "Eitel Allen Nelson's 'The Saga of Peta Nocona.'" *Southwestern Historical Quarterly* 55, no. 1 (July 1951): 118–22.

Ellison, J. W. (Bud). "Scouted on Pease River." *Frontier Times* 5, no. 3 (December 1927): 100–101.

Gelo, Daniel J. "'Comanche Land and Ever Has Been': A Native Geography of the

Nineteenth-Century Comancheria." *Southwestern Historical Quarterly* 103 (January 2000): 272–307.

Gladwin, Thomas. "Comanche Kin Behavior." *American Anthropologist* 50 (January–March 1948): 73–94.

Haley, J. Evetts, ed. "Charles Goodnight's Indian Recollections." *Panhandle-Plains Historical Review* 1 (1928): 3–29.

Holden, W. C. "Frontier Defense, 1846–1860." *West Texas Historical Association Year Book* 6 (1930): 39–71.

Hunter, J. Marvin, ed. "The Capture of Cynthia Ann Parker." *Frontier Times* 16 (May 1939): 364–65.

———. "'Uncle' Ben Dragoo, A Texas Ranger." *Frontier Times* 6, no. 7 (April 1929): 287–91.

Jones, Lawrence T., III. "Cynthia Ann Parker and Pease Ross—The Forgotten Photographs." *Southwestern Historical Quarterly* 93, no. 3 (January 1990): 379–84.

"The Killing of Chief Peta Nocona." *Frontier Times* 4, no. 3 (December 1926): 42–43.

Leupp, Francis E. "Chief Quanah Parker, The Last Great Ruler of the Comanches." *The Red Man* 3, no. 7 (March 1911): 291–96.

"Lubbock . . . Hub of the South Plains." *The Connecting Rod* 11 (August 1955): 1–3.

Nichols, J. Marvin. "The White Squaw of the Comanches." *Frontier Times* 4, no. 6 (March 1927): 44–47.

Reid, Jan. "One Who Was Found: The Legend of Cynthia Ann Parker." In *Tales of Texoma: Episodes in the History of the Red River Border*, ed. Michael L. Collins, 27–54. Wichita Falls, Texas: Midwestern State University Press, 2005.

Richardson, Rupert N., ed. "The Death of Nocona and the Recovery of Cynthia Ann Parker." *Southwestern Historical Quarterly* 46 (July 1942): 15–42.

Rickard, J. A., ed. "Recollections of B. F. Gholson." *West Texas Historical Association Year Book* 17 (1941): 108–24.

Rister, Carl Coke. "Early Accounts of Indian Depredations." *West Texas Historical Association Year Book* 1 (1926): 18–30.

Thoburn, Joseph B. "Horace P. Jones, Scout and Interpreter." *Chronicles of Oklahoma* 2, no. 4 (December 1924): 380–95.

Taulman, Araminta McClellan. "The Capture of Cynthia Ann Parker." *Frontier Times* 6, no. 8 (May 1929): 311.

"Uncle Ben Dragoo Has Colorful History." *Frontier Times* 5, no. 5 (February 1928): 216–17.

Webb, Walter Prescott. "Texas Collection." *Southwestern Historical Quarterly* 46 (July 1942): 63–74.

Wellman, Paul I. "Cynthia Ann Parker." *Chronicles of Oklahoma* 12, no. 2 (June 1934): 163–70.

Williams, Robert H. "The Case for Peta Nocona." *Texana* 10, no. 1 (1972): 55–72.

Wynne, Mamie Folsom. "History Centers about Cynthia Ann Parker's Home." *Frontier Times* 6, no. 7 (April 1929): 258–60.

# INDEX

# INDEX

# INDEX